*B*ark *If You Love Me*

Also by Louise Bernikow

The American Women's Almanac: An Inspiring & Irreverent History

Alone in America

Let's Have Lunch: Games of Sex and Power

Among Women

The World Split Open

Abel

Bark If
You Love Me

A Woman-Meets-Dog
Story

by
Louise Bernikow

Algonquin Books of Chapel Hill   2000

Published by

Algonquin Books of Chapel Hill

Post Office Box 2225

Chapel Hill, North Carolina 27515-2225

a division of

Workman Publishing

708 Broadway

New York, New York 10003

Printed in the United States of America.

Published simultaneously in Canada by Thomas Allen & Son Limited.

Design by Anne Winslow.

Library of Congress Cataloging-in-Publication Data

Bernikow, Louise, 1940–
    Bark if you love me : a woman-meets-dog story / by Louise Bernikow.
      p. cm.
    ISBN 1-56512-258-2
    1. Dogs—New York (State)—New York—Anecdotes. 2. Bernikow,
Louise, 1940– I. Title.
SF426.2.B48 2000
636.7'0887—dc21   00-056584

10 9 8 7 6 5 4 3 2 1

First Edition

For Mark Gold, who saved my life;
Honor and Deborah, who
made it worth living;
and the little brown angel
who just dropped in

"The great pleasure of a dog is that
you may make a fool of yourself with him
and not only will he not scold you,
but he will make a fool of himself too."

—SAMUEL BUTLER

Contents

PROLOGUE

· · · · · · · · · · · · · ·

I grew up aspiring to be part of a world in which things matched, where women wore cashmere sweater sets of the same hue and texture and set dinner tables with complementary china, glassware, napkins, and even centerpieces. A bookish girl, I desired a future that included a library of my own, a room with walnut ceiling-high shelves and rows of anyone's collected works in deep red leather with gold titles.

The book you are about to read revolves around a mismatch of serious proportions and the miracle of how it worked out. There are three elements in the story: a woman, a city, and a dog. The woman and the city are a natural pair, for I grew into a lover of busy, overpopulated, dense, work-absorbed, urban life. To me, the mix of races, classes, languages, looks, occupations, and attitudes made Manhattan one of the most interesting human landscapes on earth. Early on, I came to depend on street life and city culture for solace and inspiration.

A dog didn't fit the picture. Too bucolic. Animals, to my mind, belonged in the great outdoors, romping across fields at best or fetching newspapers from suburban curbs and trotting across lawns to deposit them on porches. Mom, Dad, Dick, and Jane had dogs. Not me. Not here, where I live. Not now.

I did not choose the dog; he chose me. I did not resist, for reasons as mysterious as his chance appearance on my path on a particular day. The longer I knew him, the deeper the mystery became: where he'd come from and why, how he had survived and what he had been sent— for I soon came to think of him as "sent"—to teach me.

The student was ready; the teacher appeared. The lessons were mostly about love in many guises, community in many forms, and change. The dog changed the city for me. And he changed me, beginning with a radical rethinking of what made for a good match.

Bark If You Love Me

Hot

The Rescue

·············

On the sunny brink of Memorial Day weekend, I was out for an afternoon run in Riverside Park with nothing much on my calendar for the days ahead and a lot of clutter in my mind. I'd stretched my cramping legs and darted across the Drive, crammed bumper-to-bumper with cars full of people escaping the city. My idea of a holiday was staying home, sleeping, sorting the clutter. I needed a breather.

The stone steps going down into the park reeked of canine and human piss. I exhaled at the bottom and started along the pavement, past an iron-fenced dog run with noisy nattering animals racing around, kicking up dust. On the flattened dirt path that common use had made a jogging trail, a woman of Olympian speed and musculature passed me going in the other direction, then a man and woman moving at a shuffle, hooked together to a Walkman.

The gears meshed and I finally got a stride, until a big shaggy dog chasing a yelping smaller one raced across the path, right at my feet, and almost tripped me.

"Get those dogs on a leash," I shouted irritably over my shoulder in the general direction of two people standing and talking nearby, leashes dangling from their hands instead of attached to their canines.

I recovered my balance and picked up speed, dodging a Frisbee. Sweat broke through under my arms and across my breastbone.

No more than half a mile along, a police car was stopped along the roadway. People gathered around it. This generally meant a body had been found in the park or, more rarely, a jogger hurt. Since I can't pass a hubbub without wanting to see what it's about, I stopped, took a few deep breaths, and walked over.

The cops had their windows rolled down. On the driver's side, a woman jiggled a baby in a three-wheeled canvas contraption she had been running with. Around her were several people in business clothes, a man holding two cocker spaniels on leashes, a young Asian woman with a huge long-haired dog lying like a rug at her feet, and another young woman in shorts and a Barnard College T-shirt.

I asked what was going on.

The police had a dog, the Barnard student said, who'd been found beaten, starving, tied to a tree. He needed a home. Oh, please, I thought, with all the trouble in this city, the police are out saving dogs?

"We can't have pets in the dorms," the young woman was saying, "or I'd take it." She looked tragic. It's only a dog, I thought. Get a grip. I looked over her shoulder, into the car.

He was curled like a cat, a dark brown ball with large amber eyes, huddled on the back seat. The man with the cocker spaniels was telling the cops he wanted the dog, but didn't think his girlfriend would tolerate another one. Oh, don't be such a wuss, I thought, but the man's voice was fading away, like background noise in a movie scene. The woman, baby, and contraption jogged off.

The dog looked back at me. A boxer's face, I thought, from meager experience. Flat, dark nose. Those eyes. He didn't move, just looked me over, wearily, with some curiosity. He was panting and a long pink tongue spilled from his dark, parted lips.

I WAS NOT A PERSON well acquainted with dogs or animals of any kind. No childhood memories of bounding with a tail-wagging pup over hill and dale or in the froth of the ocean's spray, no grandma's house where Lassie barked with glee at the sight of me, no beloved National Velvet colt hidden away in my heart. Politically, it made sense to save the whales, hug trees, and create humane conditions in which mare's urine could be collected for transformation into hormones for menopausal women, but I never went to the barricades over animal rights issues. Let's worry about people first, I always said. And did.

On the Bronx sidewalks of my youth and in the large apartment houses, we were not canine-friendly. We were not, in fact, nature-friendly. "Nature" was laced with dangers, like spiders, wasps, and bees. Cats gave us the willies. Dogs were more scary and dirty to boot. They jumped up on you out of nowhere. They bit. They carried disease and that dreaded stuff called allergens. My mother, whose ostensible job was to guard her pups against the world's dangers, always said I was allergic to trees, grass, and animals. Who was I, who had suffered asthmatic terrors far too often in my young years, to disagree?

In this, as in most matters, my fearful mother generalized from a small truth. Life so far had proven her only partially right. Most of the perils described to me in my childhood had never materialized. I hadn't picked up diseases from toilet seats in public bathrooms nor been found dead in the street after a car accident, wearing dirty underwear. Christians hadn't betrayed me. Men hadn't used me. I'd actually outgrown childhood problems like asthma and poor eyesight and had come to believe, like most Americans, that I'd left all limitations behind.

But I hadn't. In Los Angeles once, hobnobbing with movie people and jockeying for a deal, I'd stayed near the beach with an old friend and his two cats. The cats hadn't registered until I woke in the night, gasping. I wheezed my way out of the house, walked near the shore, inhaling intensely. Although reason said buy medicine, stay elsewhere, make the deal, I went, instead, to the airport. The ticket change was costly, but the plane was mercifully free of cat. The deal fell through.

Yet for a week or two, some summers, while my friends Alyosha and Lisa left the Berkeley hills to travel, I watched over their house and dog. Ariel, a female black and white Portuguese water spaniel, didn't make me sneeze, gasp, itch, or flee. I drove around with her sticking her nose out the car's back window. We climbed the Indian rocks and stared out at San Francisco Bay. I ran the track off The Alameda with her on a leash, perplexed about going in circles. One night, she woke me, making a racket, thumping her tail on the floor. I, who had never been able to give orders to anyone, told her firmly to stop. In the California morning, I discovered, listening to the radio, that Ariel's tail thumping had been an alert. A minor earthquake had come in the night.

But Ariel belonged to California and my relationship with her was a Pacific Coast–induced aberration, like eating sprouts or saying *freeway*. At heart, I was a New Yorker, a clotheshorse, a snob, a feminist intellectual, and a world adventurer, happier on banquettes in cafés in the great capitals of the world than in the aisles of the Home Depot. I rented places to live and had no desire to own real estate because I dreaded being anchored. I felt compelled to be ready, at all times, to leave for Paris on a moment's notice. I was not interested in collaborating or camping, baking bread or raising babies.

That's who I was or thought I was.

Then, standing in Riverside Park in Manhattan, sweating beside a police car, I did one of the strangest things I've ever done: I took the little brown dog home.

I can't say why. I looked into his eyes and I took him home, just that. I can't even quite say how. I have no memory of saying yes or of being asked anything about myself or my circumstances by the police. I can't conjure an image of the car door opening, of the dog scampering out or myself lifting him. I don't remember "good-byes" and certainly not "good lucks."

The dog was on his legs, a metal-studded dark leather collar around his neck attached to a chain with a blue cloth handle for a leash. He walked along beside me, looking small, brown, and scared, but agreeable. A posse accompanied us through the park—the Barnard student; the wimpy man with his spaniels; and an opera singer named Lisa who lives in my building and has a small dog named Baxter, both of whom had somehow joined us along the way.

There are many things I know. I can recite the prologue to *The Canterbury Tales* in Middle English, build bookcases with my own hands, change the motor oil in a car, and tell you why the ERA failed. I also do not lack for daring. But the little brown thing trotting beside me, occasionally stealing a look up, was daunting and a little scary. Was he a killer? A lunatic? Rabid? About to expire?

I had no idea how he worked. What did he eat and how often? Where would he sleep and how much? While Ariel had a yard in Berkeley to dash out to, this character's yard would be four flights down and three blocks away. How was that supposed to work?

The posse, to whom I communicated concern mostly

through looks of alarm, accompanied me and the mysterious stranger to the pet store on Broadway. It was a large, bright shop, with parrots in the window, more birds in more cages inside, leashes, toys, vitamins, fish in tanks, and a funny smell. I felt squeamish.

The posse understood, perhaps better than I, the provisional nature of my new alliance. The Barnard student chose two white plastic bowls; I liked the stainless steel. From an array of foods in bags and cans as overwhelming in variety as breakfast cereals in the supermarket or underwear at Bloomingdale's, Lisa picked out a sack of dog food allegedly made of lamb and rice. It felt suspiciously desiccated as I carried it down the aisle, along with a plastic sack of oatmeal-colored biscuits. The man with the spaniels contributed a red rubber pull toy and went home to feed his dogs. I lingered at the cosmetics, eventually choosing a citrus shampoo I wouldn't have minded using myself. The little brown dog toddled up and down the aisles compliantly. It was the last time he would behave that way in the store.

The student left us after chipping in for what she called my "starter kit" and I tried not to think of as a layette. Lisa, Baxter, the little dog, and I walked home in the evening light, two women and two dogs. Lisa was treating me like I'd joined her cult or converted to her religion.

"I'll see how it goes," I said.

"Right."

Lisa let Baxter into their first-floor apartment. She, I, and the little brown dog climbed four flights of stairs. He seemed eager and curious. Up he went and up again, not complaining. He waited while I unlocked the door and then he led me into my own apartment. Lisa set the bowls down in a corner of the kitchen and began running water in the sink.

No, I said, I'll do it.

She had something like a smirk on her face.

WE WERE ALONE. IGNORING me, the dog dipped his head and guzzled the water. I filled the second bowl to the brim with brown nuggets of alleged lamb and rice from the food sack and stepped away. He sucked up the food, chomped, spilled dry bits on the floor, guzzled some more. I watched him. His coat was not just dark brown, but striped with black ripples — brindled, I would learn — the color of maple ice cream and fudge ripple or of pumpernickel bagels. There were splashes of white around his toenails and a white triangle on his chest, like a Superman insignia. His ears were long and floppy, his tail stumpy, with a bare spot at the end. He had a comic face — beautiful wide eyes set close together, a flat black nose, and blubbery, clownish lips.

His body was pitifully sunken in at the chest and the sides, ribs showing, as though someone had let the air out of him. And he was a boy. I may have asked or noticed when I first encountered him in the police car, but it only registered now—registered in a way that made me nervous—that there was a penis in my house. Again.

I was in a somewhat nunnish phase. Behind me lay many years of experience in all parts of the globe with many kinds of "others." I'd been, I thought, a dashing adventuress for a time—and a joyous time it was—and then I'd set up housekeeping with a graphic artist I'd known for many years. We eventually separated, amicably—except for feral fights over, oddly enough, ownership of a pair of poultry shears. After that, I became the kind of single woman proud of earning her own living, appalled at ever being asked to break a date with a woman friend for a man. I spent many years in furtive passion and a failed attempt to pry what I thought was the love of my life away from a marriage to someone else. Eventually, I fell for an adorable, sexy, smart, and talented young man named Peter, who kept me laughing for nearly a decade while I played grown-up. He'd been gone for some time.

I was now a single woman in New York in the nineties, only this time around it had lost its edge. This time, living alone was unremarkable. I worked, hung out, went out, connected, and bedded, still, but only one toothbrush stood on my bathroom shelf. If love wanted to claim me again, I thought, it would have to knock very loudly, because I wasn't looking or listening for it. Things were fine as they were.

Then, on Memorial Day weekend, I had, as my fearful mother worried I would, and not for the first time, gone blithely into the world and come home with a strange male. Most of the other strange males I'd lured or dragged home had been labeled immediately. I knew Peter was a keeper after our first dinner together. Others were conditional (if he does this or that, he can stay), transients, or outright rejects. This one was a mystery.

He stared at me. I stared back. I noticed that I wasn't sneezing or itchy, nor was I afraid. Wary, yes, enough to keep him collared and leashed, but not alarmed—an interesting bit of faith or stupidity on my part, since he'd come in off the street with no polite introduction or breeder's credentials.

"Sit down," I said, tentatively.

He sat on the wood floor immediately and rather awkwardly, one leg tucked in, the other jutting straight out, a yoga posture. I didn't know his name, his background, his age, his health, his temperament, or even what language he spoke. From the police story—tied to a tree and abandoned, they'd said—and from the look of him, he'd been through something awful. He'd need a lot, beginning with a name.

I dropped the leash and walked into my writing room, with its well-worn couch, shelves of hardcovers and paperbacks, stacks of newspapers and magazines on the coffee table and the floor, a small sculpture, prints, posters on the wall.

The dog followed me, leash chain clanking and tail wagging. This, I told him, is the most important part of the house. This is sacred ground. Be very careful. He sniffed but did not topple a stack of magazines.

"Good boy," I said.

I went to my desk. He followed.

"Sit down," I said again.

He sat on the floor, in the same odd position. I sat in my chair and picked up the phone.

What do I do now? I asked the universe.

Help!

. . . .

"I've found a dog. What do I do now?" I asked the woman who answered the phone at the ASPCA. I listened and answered her questions:

"It's a male. No, there are no tags."

"Is he neutered?"

"I don't know. How can you tell?"

"He won't have any testicles." I heard her sigh and maybe even repress a giggle.

"Oh no. I can't look *down there*. I just met him."

But I did and he didn't. Still, it felt like an invasion of his privacy to be peeking at his genitals. I wouldn't want him to do that to me. My ideas about equality didn't disappear simply because the "other" was another species. His eyes bespoke a soul and a personality; he deserved my respect.

I made an appointment for the next day, then canceled my dinner plans for that evening, saying only that something important had come up. In my world, deadlines, illness, exhaustion, and, sometimes, divorces, breakups, or falling in love, were acceptable reasons for breaking dates with friends. Not, "I brought a dog home and don't want to leave him alone his first night."

I showed him the outdoor terrace, lined with planter boxes of struggling herbs and the beginnings of columbine, irises, and clematis. I held his leash, lest he jump over the low walls or think he was back in the park and pee. Then I returned to the living room, got an old comforter out of a closet and made a bed for him on the floor, near the pedestal oak table.

"Lie down," I said.

Dragging his leash, he came over and lay down. I tied the leash around the pedestal.

I sat on the couch with a book, looking up every paragraph or so. At first, he just looked back at me, then he put his head down. His eyes closed, but not completely. He looked like a scrawny, wet, and potentially epileptic muskrat.

I tiptoed out of the room and went to bed. It was very quiet. It was too quiet. I got up and crept back to where he slept. He looked up. I went back to bed. I got up. Maybe, if I kept him, I'd need an intercom, the kind new parents get when the baby comes home.

In the early morning light, he was still alive, not tangled and strangled in the leash, his ribs still pumping in and out. I knelt beside him as he rose and licked my lips. Our first kiss. Wet. Then he hit me. Boxed me, right paw raised to tap my shoulder and on his face an expression that said, Get it?

I got it. With my pocket full of paper towels, we lumbered down four flights of stairs and into the street, where I finally noticed how crooked his right back leg was and how little weight he put on it. The skinny leg was turned out like a ballet dancer's in first position, the knee joint swollen. His walk was lopsided, like Marilyn Monroe with a bit sliced off the heel of one shoe to give her some sway.

Maybe he'd cramped it in his sleep, but I didn't think so. My heart twinged. I imagined a collapse, ambulance, surgery, pain, and mounting medical bills. I looked around, as though the police car might magically reappear and I could give him back. Sorry, I'd say, mea culpa, I'm not very good at this. Let's put the past twenty-four hours on rewind and I'll keep jogging in the park, pass the car without stopping, take a shower, go out, and have my life to myself again. I wasn't cruel, only traumatized, having recently suffered, along with my father and brother, my mother's slow, awful death from congestive heart failure. Neither St. Francis nor Florence Nightingale were roles I aspired to or felt equipped for.

But the dog suddenly took off, back legs pumping, racing along the street like a husky in the Alaskan wilderness, with me as the sled. He zigzagged from curb to stoop to tree, braking to lift his leg, always the right one, balancing on the left, pissing a huge stream, then careening off again, until we came to West End Avenue, where he stopped and looked up, waiting for orders to proceed.

I'd crossed a line. To passersby—an early morning jogger in tank top and shorts, a teenager on a bike, a gray-haired man carrying a Starbucks bag, the super setting garbage cans at the curb up the street—I was now a person with a dog, an out-of-control person and a hyperactive dog, a dog person, like those I myself had skirted along these very same sidewalks only the day before. On my side of the line, I flushed with embarrassment when he crouched in the middle of the sidewalk, a bright red lipstick emerging from between his legs and small turds dropping to the concrete. How could I respect the privacy of someone who didn't respect his own?

Awkwardly, I swiped the paper towels and scanned the street for horrified onlookers and a trash can, in that order. A woman with a large black poodle nodded and kept walking. Two kids bouncing a basketball back and forth didn't even look back. The dog's lipstick retracted and there was a trash can on the corner.

Our appointment at the ASPCA was for that morning and still he lacked a name. Surely they'd ask. He couldn't be Dog Doe. I was blankly trying to think of a name while I opened the apartment door. Something literary and masculine. Whitman? The dog wasn't a Yankee; there was something of another culture about him. Byron? Less Anglo.

He ran into the apartment and I let him go. Gathering keys and checkbook, I heard him in the kitchen, slurping at the water bowl. The sound stopped. I went to look. He'd gone into my writing room.

He lay on the couch, head on paws.

"Off," I said. How did I know these things?

He didn't move, but he did wiggle his tail ferociously.

"Off." And don't touch the books. *Les livres sont interdits. No toca los libros.*

Libro! I'd never heard of a dog named Libro.

Libro for "book." In Spanish, for something Latino about him, about the street life in our neighborhood, and about me, a woman unaccountably at home in Spain and in the language of Lorca, St. Theresa, and flamenco. Libro's name was so original it lessened the chances of calling to him only to have nine spaniels, two Labs, and a dalmatian come running.

Libro it was.

We left for the ASPCA. At the corner of West End Avenue, three taxis in a row sped by, refusing to stop. I hid Libro behind my legs, but another cab slowed and then roared off when he saw the dog. We were late. I got the next cab that passed to stop by waving frantically, the old damsel-in-distress act, and saying to the driver: "He has to go to the doctor. And he's very well behaved." Like I knew.

Libro huddled on my lap. I remembered Ariel's head hanging merrily out the window in the Berkeley hills, but that was another dog, another place. I stroked his head. He licked my hand. I wondered if he'd ever traveled in a car before and vowed to try to take him as he was, not make him live in Ariel's shadow. If he stayed.

The ASPCA waiting room reminded me of an airport —molded plastic chairs, fluorescent lights, TV mounted on the wall, blaring. It was crowded with people, coupled or alone, old and young, with dogs and cats in all shapes, sizes, and conditions, straining at leashes, lying on the floor or cradled in someone's arms, in cardboard boxes, or carriers. I was the only white person.

Libro, dragging me, made a beeline for a young black man, whose German shepherd lay quietly at his feet, paw bandaged with a piece of sheet. The dog growled. Libro backed off. The man spoke quietly to the shepherd, who put his head down on his paws and watched Libro nuzzle the man's leg and lick his hand.

A jealous shiver went down my spine. It occurred to me for the first time that the people Libro had lived with might turn up somewhere, anywhere, and want him back. Never, I said to myself, leading Libro away from man and shepherd, neither having recognized him. His abuser deserved jail.

By the time we got to see a doctor, Libro had been much admired by the waiting people, some of their dogs, and none of their cats. I'd talked with an elderly couple with a large dog lying very still in a cut-down cardboard box at their feet. She was a tan-and-white female pit bull who'd given birth and been put out in the street immediately afterward, which raised my hackles. The box said "Pampers" on the side.

The female vet weighed Libro in at twenty-eight pounds and guessed his age at close to a year. He licked her face and took his shots like a man. I asked if his vocal cords were okay, since he hadn't made a single sound since I'd brought him home. She thought they were, but otherwise, he was a medical mess, needing care for infected ears and eyes and a great deal of further investigation about his bad leg.

Had he been beaten? The vet couldn't say. Often, she said, boxers suffer from hip dysplasia, but he seemed young for that. As he did for arthritis. She ran her fingers down his leg, feeling for swelling or breaks. He looked away, but didn't wince. Then the vet had Libro walk down the flourescent-drenched hallway and back while she watched with narrowed eyes. His walk was gimpy, his return, at a gallop, floppy-eared and fluid.

Did I want his leg X-rayed?

I had two concerns. My checkbook was one. The other was what I understood of Libro's "state." I'd never made health care decisions for anyone else and few enough for my own robust self, but I was sure he had endured enough for the moment. He needed to recover from the trauma, I believed, not undergo more poking and prodding. Unless—I turned, insecurely, to the vet— his problem was urgent.

The vet thought not. No use doing an X ray, she told me, unless I was prepared to go ahead with surgery, if he needed it. Use aspirin judiciously, for pain, she advised, and give it a few months.

I was optimistic. Am, anyway, but have learned to counter my own tendency to hypochondria with platitudes like, "It's probably nothing" and "Most things are better by morning."

I bought eye ointment, ear cleaner, a prophylactic pill for heartworm, and something to smear on his shoulders to keep fleas and ticks away. I signed papers making him legitimate; the temporary license tag got hooked into his collar.

We headed home, meandering several miles from the edge of Manhattan's east side, through Central Park, to its western boundary. It was a warm, sunny afternoon. Libro stopped to rest every once in a while, lying down in a shady spot with an apologetic look on his face, like my old grandma used to have when we were out walking and she was sorry to be slowing me down. Midpark, we passed tennis courts packed with players, surrounded by benches where dozens more waited their turn. I would have liked to be out playing, but I had a dog with me. I remembered Peter at this same spot, red leather jacket over white tennis clothes, saying I wanted too much and he was leaving. A month later, he moved in.

Libro, who had moved in without hesitation, knew some surprising things. He had apparently arrived in my life with the software already installed. Without instruction from me, he stopped at streetcorners, waited, and then, on command, hurried across. Also without instruction and as a result of my failure to carry libations for a hot day, he found water fountains in the park, stood up, and guzzled. This, I would learn, was illegal. He had the mind of a felon.

I knew nothing, except that my bank balance was lighter and my pockets were stuffed with pills and ointments. The conversation I was having with him in my head went something like: you're just going to have to show me what you need; look here, I'm not much of a mom, but I'm a great pal; and please don't bite anybody.

Like most New Yorkers, I avoid eye contact in public. Living too close to each other, we urban citizens maintain our privacy by creating "personal space" in crowds. Also, as Libro was already showing me, a direct stare is an act of aggression. But I was out walking with a born charmer. He had his ways of attracting the attention of most people and dogs that we passed. I engaged many strangers that afternoon.

"What a beautiful dog."

Libro stood there, accepting but a little bored, like some movie stars I've seen.

I said "Thank you."

"What's wrong with his leg?"

"Somebody beat him up."

The person's eyes considered an indictment against me. I felt compelled to dismiss it. "Not me," I said, hurriedly.

"Hiya, girl."

"He's a boy!"

"What's his name?"

"Libro."

"Oh, was he born in October? My sister's a Libra too."

"*Libro*. It means book in Spanish."

I'd never noticed how much stuff lay around the city's sidewalks, but on our way across town, Libro investigated and watered empty plastic bags in all sizes and colors, coffee cups, a tennis shoe, many stacks of magazines, a man's tie, a sketchbook, a pair of jeans, a sun visor, a torn window screen, dirty tennis balls, clean tennis balls, and a few collapsed balloons.

On Central Park West, I found a child's pink straw hat on the ground and playfully set it on his head. He shook it off. I tried again and he hurled it away, head ducking like a bull. His first act of defiance. No more doggy nice guy. No hats. Or no girls' hats? He wasn't a stuffed toy for me to pick up when I was lonely and put down when I had to save the world or earn a buck or for me to dress up in silly stuff for my own amusement. I looked at him with new respect.

When we got home, he went slowly, in obvious pain, up the four flights of stairs. He ate, kissed my face, and slept on the comforter. I called my father.

"You have a what?"

"Well, I have this dog, but I'm not sure I'm going to keep him."

"You know," my father said, clearly striving for his life-long balance between embrace and admonition, "you have to take care of them."

I'd already figured that out.

My two closest friends doubted not my sanity, but my veracity. Rosemary, tall, rich, born WASP, but rebel-lious, lives single in a Revolutionary War saltbox in the country with a dog of her own. "You couldn't possibly," she said, perhaps meaning, I thought later, that I wasn't allowed to have a dog because she had one. Sibling ri-valry. Diana, dogless, married, urban shrink, said, "No you don't."

I called my brother and current sister-in-law. He re-minded me that he'd had a dog in one of his other mar-riages (more sibling rivalry) and she said, "Great. It's a good way to meet people," by which she meant men.

Good Neighbors

....

Libro and I kept to ourselves for two days before venturing into Riverside Park. I wanted to solidify the relationship. Twice a day, I sat on the floor beside him while he ate, messily, huge mouthfuls of food only partially swallowed, pellets slipping onto the floor. Well, I told him, Peter used to say I needed to be hosed down after a meal. I chalk it up to enthusiasm. He slurped and dribbled his water. He licked my face.

He scratched his left ear violently, but I knew what to do. He'd gone into my office again, jumped on the sofa, been shooed off, and was lying on the floor. I knelt beside him, ear medication and cotton pads in hand. He didn't flinch. Squirting the medication into one ear made him shiver, shake, get up, and pace around, but he came back. I medicated the other ear and he kissed my face.

But he also had panic attacks, running around the apartment, panting hard, his eyes wide and terrified. Some afternoons, curled on his quilt, napping, his eyes flipped open and closed fast and his whole body shivered and spasmed. I didn't know what to do about doggy nightmares.

"Hang on," I whispered. "It'll get better."

OUT WE FINALLY WENT into the heart of the local civilization of dogs and their people. Down the street we sped, across the Drive—so empty of cars now it looked like a pedestrian boulevard—and down the stone steps. Libro limped badly and occasionally hopped on three legs. But fun and comradeship had been great tonics for me and so I hoped they would be so for him.

The dog run was a fenced corral, dirt-and-wood-chip-floored, with a few benches. Dogs were racing around and people were clustered in groups, with the occasional oddball off by him or herself, reading a book, ignoring the world. It felt like walking into a high school cafeteria midway into the school year, when the cliques have long ago been formed.

I have lived in the same neighborhood for three decades. I have gone door-to-door here for political candidates. I've gotten mugged, voted, chased down a robber, kissed several lovers, and carried groceries, newspapers, and videos through the streets. I've jogged in Riverside Park, walked to the clay tennis courts at 97th Street and the hard courts at 120th, moved a parked car from the restricted side of the street before 8 A.M. and back three hours later. I've watched the tall ships sail up the Hudson, pointed out the house William Randolph Hearst built for Marion Davies long before it had a landmark sign—usually adding, "that was in the days when being a mistress meant you got a mansion."

The neighborhood is home, dense with my history. The New Yorker Bookstore, a great place to pick up guys, and the movie theater, which showed "art house" movies, have been replaced. Now we have a Barnes and Noble superstore—a great place to meet better dressed, richer, and more shallow men, who don't even pretend to look at the books—and a new multiplex, where "art" means the kiss of death. The butcher who once told me it was a shame a pretty girl like me was buying dinner for one is long gone. The video rental store, where Peter used to carry on—"oh no, don't make me watch the one with the sheep again"—has moved to larger quarters across the street. But the Fairway market, with its bins of glistening produce, is still there and thriving, and so is Zabars, where tour buses sometimes stop to show visitors the bliss of chopped liver. So am I.

In all that time and during all those activities, I had never seen any of the people now clustered in the dog run.

"How old is he?" they asked, the doggy world equivalent of the cocktail party opener, "And what do you do?"

I recited my litany: he's almost a year old, his name is Libro, that means book, in Spanish, and some creep, not me, hurt his leg, so he's been rescued.

There was not a Spot among the local canines, but many highfalutin names: Athena, the chocolate Lab; Samson and Delilah, young rottweilers; two Rexes and a Bishop; an Emma named after Emma Bovary; a Tiggy for Antigone; a Winnie who looked like Churchill. There was an occasional smattering of pop culture dogs, like Elvis and Gracie, both gray-and-white sheepdogs, living in different households. I was hardly the first person — judging from the owner's indulgent expression — to say "Goodnight, Gracie."

If I'd dared try matching dogs and the people who lived with them, I would have failed miserably. There seemed no logic to the pairings in the run. Samson and

Delilah lived with a thirtyish, well-toned actor; Athena with a jolly male public relations executive; a delicate Japanese breed named Mercy with a woman psychoanalyst. There were big people with small dogs; average-sized humans with mammoth canines, like the huge white Great Dane who was deaf; and little apparent correlation between men/women, straight/gay, single/coupled and the gender or breed that shared their lives.

Not that I knew beans about breeds. Libro was Libro, but he was also a boxer. There was something only vaguely pugilistic about his face, the flat nose especially, and I could see that he might punch a little with one or the other of his front legs, but *boxer* meant no more to me than *palomino* might mean to a kid who only wanted a pony ride. A dog is a dog is a dog, I thought.

The single exception to my inability to discern a match between dog and person was the chubby man in the run, hovering over his overweight spaniel, keeping up a continual monologue: "No, Ollie. No sticks. Drop it, Ollie. Good boy. No, Ollie. No dirt. Sit, Ollie. Good boy." Every time Ollie sat, he got a treat and also got his nose wiped with a handkerchief from the man's pocket. They seemed right together.

Aswirl in dust, surrounded by orchestral barking, ointment in his eyes, medication in his ears, but surprisingly agile, dashing around on four legs, Libro was profligate in his attentions. He boxed the large white Great Dane and ran away. He got down on his belly near a little Japanese-looking dog and licked her nose when she approached. He chased Athena, the Lab. He got especially cozy with a little Portuguese water spaniel named Josie, about his age. The relief I felt at his social aptitude must also sweep over moms watching toddlers on the first day of nursery school or day care.

My life among the dog people would come to include more people and dogs than I could ever name, and most of the humans would remain as anonymous as the folks in any twelve-step basement meeting. For all I knew, like the people in the basements, they could be pickpockets or physicists, so totally leveled was the canine playing field. But Josie's owners made an impression from the beginning.

He wrote mysteries and she had taught at MIT. They were full of sophisticated and esoteric canine lore, more difficult for me to grasp than calculus. They fed their dog foods I had never heard of, had opinions about which toys were useful for her to play with, carried nutritious treats, and were about to start training her with a clicker, whatever that was. I was a little daunted by them, but not by Josie, who reminded me of California Ariel and was quite the tomboy, holding her own in a pack of male dogs, a girl after my own heart.

The man who lived with Athena told me how she had dragged a newspaper down off the dining room table to use as a toilet when he was late getting home. Josie's people talked about her heritage and pedigree. A prickly, braggy, doggy pride took hold of me. "Last night," I said, "when I gave Libro his first bath, he climbed right into the tub and stood there, no trouble at all. Then he put first one paw, then the other, into my hand. I think he wanted a pedicure."

I didn't tell them how afraid I'd been about touching him all over, how gingerly I'd used the washcloth on his hindquarters. I didn't say I was wary of his penis.

The pedicure request was yet another clue that Libro, despite his recent trauma, was accustomed to being well treated. A plot line was forming in my mind: dog has a happy home, then something violent intervenes and he ends up a mess, beaten and abandoned. A drug story? Marital two-timing and Sicilian-style vengeance? A theft? I checked out the mystery writer. He was busy watching Josie grab another dog's leash and try to lead it out of the dog run. Atta girl! Nope, I'd solve this one myself.

The gate swung open and in came a sleek tan dog and a nattily dressed black man. Libro and Josie charged over together, but only Libro stayed to connect. If I'd had a movie camera, I'd have panned the whole run, a dozen or more big and small canines in various stages of activity or rest, and come in fast for a close-up of Libro and the ginger-colored dog. The muted barking on the sound track would die down and up would swell Rachmaninoff or Chopin.

The new arrival's green eyes looked determinedly off into the distance. Libro's were fixed on her. She ran off, he followed, she averted her eyes, his were glued to her. They looked like Bill and Hillary on Inauguration Day, with Libro playing First Lady. Lola, her name was, and vizsla her breed, according to the man who escorted her. Shorthaired and muscular like Libro, she was clearly in the business of chasing prey. He was apparently in the business of seducing her. Libro was in love.

I was a fish out of water, a discord, to start with, in the dressing department. Except for the man with Lola, sockless in moccasins, wearing neatly pressed khaki walking shorts and a well-fitting Calvin Klein black T-shirt, everybody else was scruffy. It was a cutoffs, baseball cap, and running-shoes-with-athletic-socks crowd. I was in a short DKNY halter-top dress and sandals, as "inappropriate" to the situation as the white suit Jackie Kennedy once wore on a campaign trip to the coal mines of West Virginia.

Beware of activities for which you need a new wardrobe. I had nothing to wear for life with a dog because my closet, like my life, had·been recently transformed. It had taken a long time to let go of the things Peter left behind. I'd found one of his T-shirts in the clothes hamper and worn it to bed for a week. The photograph of us in its silver frame stayed on the mantel over the fireplace. Almost a year later, friends forced me to pack all the pictures and scribbled love notes into a box and put that in the closet. Actually, they said in the garbage, but closet was the closest I could come. While I was at it, I had cleaned out every doesn't-quite-make-it, ripped-hem, button-missing, too-eighties, too-bohemian piece of clothing I owned. For summer, I'd kept white linen, delicate sandals, and tennis clothes, in traditional white.

Just then, Libro ceased his pursuit of Lola to reestablish his connection to me. He jumped up and licked my bare arms, leaving a trail of dusty paw prints on my linen sundress and sticky goo slobber on my skin.

It was not a natural fit, myself and the dog, myself and the dog world, in other ways as well. My voice was wrong. Others addressed their canines in high tones and cloying diminutives: "sweetie" and "baby," from men as well as women. Everybody was the "owner" of his or her dog or, worse, the "daddy" or "mommy." Now, there are not too many things that make me sick to my stomach.

Calves' brains is one and I can't remember the others. But doggy imperialism and sentimentality definitely started a churn in my intestines. I hardly "owned" Libro, surely not the way I "owned" my computer, my dishes, or my books. Clingy though he was, I could see in his eyes that he owned himself. And that he belonged in the category of God's creatures, whatever that meant. I'd signed papers whose meaning I took to be that I would care for him. I was his custodian, a temporary one at that.

As for mommy: he was a dog, I wasn't. I wondered about his family, but never presumed to be one of them. Also, single motherhood had always seemed to me one of the most heroic and difficult undertakings around. Wasn't my style. I might care for him, but not convert for him.

"Yo! Libro!"

I had to call several times before he took his eyes off Lola.

"Yo! Libro!" again. I've never been able to whistle.

No mommy talk here. He wasn't my baby, but he was the leading candidate for new best friend. Not *madre* and *niño*, but Butch and Sundance maybe, sidekicks. I swaggered out of the dog run. He limped.

LIBRO MADE FRIENDS FAST, especially among the neighbors. It was not just myself suddenly living with a dog, but all the people in my building, none of whom had a choice about it.

Nick, Reece, and Andy, Columbia graduate students in the next door apartment, had come from west of the Mississippi to make it big in New York. They slept late, threw out large piles of beer bottles, cooked a lot of pasta, and, judging from what I heard through the walls, watched a lot of sports on television. I'd seen them the day they moved in with futons and skis and then at different times of day or night, on the staircase. Andy went up and down the four flights in his roller blades. When asked, I'd given them hints about local laundries and bagel shops, and about once every two weeks, one of them, in T-shirt and jeans, would knock at my door and ask to borrow the vacuum cleaner. About the third time that happened, Nick came back to admit, sheepishly, that he'd broken it. In fact, he'd only overfilled the vacuum bag. I changed it. I was trying hard not to become the den mother.

Andy in his roller blades first met an ebullient Libro on the staircase and nearly lost his footing. Nick was introduced immediately afterward, when Andy opened the door to their apartment and the dog rushed in, sniffing, straight to a bed where Nick was tucked up in his sleeping bag. We almost never saw Reece, who had a waiter's job in addition to a full school schedule. The boys, as I thought of them, had all grown up in more wide-open spaces, with nature as a congenial part of the landscape, and they took to Libro with a Huck Finn–like ease I envied. Andy in particular, who missed his childhood dogs, seemed to know exactly where to rub and scratch. I was still wary.

There were no children in our building, a situation representing the landlord's hope for turnover among renters. Some of us had dug our heels in, refusing to turn over.

Charles, a Juilliard graduate turned stockbroker, lived on the third floor. He not only played with Libro when he saw him on the staircase, but talked to him, making high-pitched dog sounds so appealing that Libro actually answered. When he played his piano, Libro sat on the doorstep, ear to the ground.

Next door to Charles were Sophia and Ted. Sophia, whom Peter used to call *la bella regazza*, was the only woman I knew who stayed home and cooked every day. She could caulk a bathtub and plaster a wall and had cemented my affection by coming upstairs and killing a huge waterbug in my bathroom, while I cowered yards away. Her husband, Ted, was an English professor. Sophia kept her distance from Libro, although she did say you could see in his eyes that he had a soul. Ted never let on how he felt.

One of three uniformed doormen in the tall, redbrick elevator building at the corner was Spanish, with a mournful El Greco face. Sometimes, he worked in shirt-sleeves, leaving the navy jacket with gold braid inside on a chair. He liked to rub and scratch Libro's whole body and got a face licking in return, but he was a little melodramatic about the leg.

"Oh, *pobrecito*," he'd moan, "poor, beautiful boy" and he'd cluck his tongue the way my grandma used to, to indicate what a great shame this was.

"Don't worry," I'd say, "he'll get better."

Carlos, the super in one of the smaller buildings down the street, wasn't quite so compassionate. Libro yanked me along, past where Carlos was cleaning up trash spilled onto the sidewalk by treasure seekers rummaging in the garbage cans. Libro stopped and wiggled his tail. Carlos kept cleaning. Libro, fast growing accustomed to being admired, looked at me, looked at Carlos, wiggled faster, and tried to get closer. Carlos froze and backed away.

Not Phoenix, a black-haired one-year-old girl who lived in the brownstone next door. She traveled in a carrier worn by her doctor mom or her dad, and her eyes lit up when she saw the pup. His, too, when he saw her. But his major connection to the world, apparently, came not from looking, but from smelling and tasting. He liked

Phoenix's bare feet very much, and although I cringed, her parents thought it cute that Libro leaped up to lick her soles and toes.

On the corner of West End Avenue, an old Irish doorman who wore a white tennis sweatband on his head greeted us every morning: "How are you today and how's the boy?"

People I'd seen in the neighborhood for years but never spoken to stopped as I walked with Libro along the overheated streets, buying a newspaper, tying him outside the bagel shop, ambling on West End Avenue, hugging the shady side of the street. Many people said they'd grown up with boxers or their grandmothers had boxers, which made me feel rather retro, the kid still in stretch pants on the ski slope while everyone else wore microfiber. They were warm, the boxer *aficionados*, but concerned. The dog looked skinny. And what was wrong with his leg?

AT 106TH STREET, WHERE West End Avenue and Broadway join up, is Straus Park, named for Ida and Isador, who went down with the Titanic. It's a triangle of plantings, benches, and a huge white marble fountain with running water, where Libro had already developed the habit of refreshing himself.

Midday, it was crowded: some older people in wheel

chairs nodding while their attendants read newspapers; teenaged lovers embracing; people on lunch breaks from the copy shop or the liquor store; and a few trim, aerobicized moms munching salads from plastic containers. Three dark-skinned women of middle age, responsible looking nannies, sat on benches rocking large carriages in which white infants slept or fretted. The women's voices lilted with the sound of the West Indies. A white woman in shorts and a halter top was stretched out at the edge of the fountain. A pale young boy and even paler, younger girl played with pails nearby.

Libro trotted up, tongue flapping. The children giggled. The woman fooled around with him and he licked her face. The boy wanted to hold his leash. The young girl reached out to pat his head. Sweet.

Libro jumped into the fountain and lifted his head under the spout. The children jumped in too and splattered him with water, which he shook off. But our pleasure was interrupted by the shouts of one of the nannies on the bench.

"Get away from that dog!"

"Nina, come here," the nanny said, rising from the bench, "Leave that dirty dog alone."

Libro looked startled. The girl froze.

The nanny charged over and grabbed the startled

Nina, picking her up with one hand; the boy sat down in the water, wide-eyed.

"Get that dog out of here," the nanny yelled at me.

"Why the hell should she? The dog ain't hurtin' anyone," the white woman in shorts screamed. She was standing on one side of me, the nanny on the other. I thought a knife fight might break out.

The nanny dragged the children back to the bench, where her friends glared at me. The woman in shorts stood there, screaming insults. I cowered on the lip of the fountain, Libro quivering against my leg.

Finally, the white woman stalked off, shouting over her shoulder, "You should go back to your own country. This is America. Fuck you."

It got very quiet, although just a few feet away, cars and trucks rumbled down Broadway. The sun beat on my face. Libro took another drink, but kept looking back, checking for explosions. I couldn't just walk away.

The women on the bench still glared. The little girl was crying.

"I'm sorry," I said to the nanny. I meant sorry about dog-loving and racist white women. "Why are you worried about the dog?"

I didn't think she would answer, but she did.

"I'm afraid he's gonna bite," she said, coldly.

Although I was on shaky ground, with only a bit more than a week of his acquaintanceship, I told her he never would, that he was the friendliest dog in New York. *En-shallah*, I added, to myself.

She said the children's mother didn't like their faces being licked by dogs. I did understand the need to obey a boss's orders. And that nothing I could say, nor any amount of charm on Libro's part, would make this moment all right. The children were back in the fountain as Libro and I left.

Until then, the only trouble I'd ever had in the neighborhood was with the old lady in the apartment next door, who smoked heavily and liked to keep the door open, to air her place out. It aired into mine. We'd had the kind of all-out war that for country people usually ends with the construction of six-foot fences and the occasional threat with a shotgun. But our battle ended by default when the old lady went to a nursing home. She'd have hated the dog.

So, Libro, I said, as we dashed over the burning asphalt, back to the air-conditioning, life with you is not entirely a bed of roses.

El Perro Es Tu Amigo

. . . .

Life was less fraught in the dog run, where Libro palled around with Josie and Athena, but abandoned them the minute Lola arrived. Like a nursery school playground, the place was full of concerned citizens who eyed Libro's crooked leg and gave me advice for healing what ailed him. He should stay off the leg. He should use it. I should soak it. I should rub it. He should have vitamins, especially E, and minerals, especially calcium. He should have fresh meat. I should cook for him. He should have acupuncture, surgery, therapy, passive exercise, aspirin, medication, hypnosis, and a consult with a psychic.

The only one who didn't offer advice was Jennifer, a gray-haired woman in her fifties who had problems of her own—a troublesome husband, two difficult sons, and a black border collie named Blackie. Woman and dog were always in some kind of fix. One day, Jennifer's arm was in a sling. She'd fallen. The next day, Blackie had a cut on his ear. One of Jennifer's sons ran away. He came back. Her husband went off on drunken benders. He came back. She never noticed Libro's limp.

I thought he should have love. When he barked or whimpered, I hugged him. Experts be damned, I said, other people back off, we'll work things out our way, not only the healing, but the living. We'll be individual, outrageous, like Josephine Baker and her cheetah on the Champs-Elysées. Champagne baths at midnight, a winter week in St. Bart's, couch potato weekends, whatever we fancy.

During those first weeks, what we fancied—or what Libro fancied and I indulged—were meals together, or my company at his meals, which numbered two and occurred at various times of the morning and evening. Routine has never been my strong suit. In rebellion, still, against a childhood of stifling repetitions—high school assembly days on Wednesday with white blouses, we always do this on Sunday, we always take that road to get to that place

—I embrace variety and spontaneity. If Libro stayed with me, he'd accommodate my schedule, which was, at best, erratic. So the morning bowl of dog food was set down on the green kitchen floor sometime between eight and ten, but the evening meal could be anytime. Whatever the clock said, though, it was our time.

I put the bowl on the floor. He gobbled. I said "slow down." He gobbled anyway, looking up anxiously to check that I was still there, putting his face in the bowl again. There was something disturbingly frantic about the way he ate; it reminded me of friends from big families who grew up fearful that all the food would be taken by others if they didn't eat fast. We have enough, I told him. "Slow down."

And I told him about my day: played phone tag with my agent, wrote three good pages and one bad one. He didn't care. Lamented the romantic miseries of one friend who had a husband and a lover, another friend who had neither. Still, he kept his head in the bowl. Heard a talk at Columbia about the end of postmodernism. Libro looked up, head cocked, listening with great seriousness.

I liked looking at him when he wasn't looking at me. In spite of the battered, scarred leg, its thigh muscle so small I could almost encircle it with thumb and forefinger, he was beautifully made. I especially liked the parts where thigh joined rump and neck merged to shoulder. He cried out for sculpting.

From my mouth came words hardly suited to thoughts of power and muscularity. "Pumpkin," I called him, or, more honestly, "punkin." "Little guy." "Baby cakes." Words I didn't know I knew, treacle, everything I detest, as though I'd visited the well of universal dog owners' psyches and come back with the cheapest stuff available.

I entrusted Libro with the secret of my gibberish and behaved in a more sophisticated manner when we were in public. He, on the other hand, behaved like a dog. On the streets, day or night, our growing intimacy evaporated. He rocked and rolled. He waddled. From a certain point of view—when he was crookedly running toward me—he had a Charlie Chaplin walk, a cockeyed Little Tramp with a twinkle in his eye. He was a poet and a one-man band, nose up, sniffing, then down, sniffing, neck stretched, ears flapping. He was at the curb, then darting across to a building, mesmerized or enchanted by the coffee cup lids, pizza crusts, cigarette packs, and torn telephone bills. If, at the streetcorner, waiting to cross, I leaned over and scratched his chin or patted his flank, he looked at me, if he looked at all, as though I were tuna fish. It was like walking in the street with a married man afraid of being caught.

I WASN'T PARANOID; there were cliques among the dog people in the park. And cliques among the dogs. There were dogs who didn't get along and people who didn't get along, unrelated to how the canines felt. There were grudges going back years, usually involving stolen toys or balls and perceived slights. The dogs operated on instinct; so did the people, but they made up reasons.

There were morning people, daytime people, evening people. We joined the morning people. Park rules were that dogs were to be leashed at all times, except when they were in the dog run, but those rules were either relaxed or overlooked until nine in the morning, when dogs ran free.

It looked like nothing less than a Brueghel landscape. Dogs everywhere. Greyhounds; Akitas; many kinds of spaniels; Labs in black, white, or brown; Porties; collies; Danes; big lumbering dogs and tiny froufrous—they cavorted on the paths that ran parallel to the river, including the paved road where I'd met Libro in the police car and the dirt jogging trail where I used to curse the canines. The dogs raced around the sloping, grassy hills in twos or threes or packs of eight. The humans, many dressed for a day at the office, carried cardboard cups of coffee with open lids, newspapers under their arms, the dogs' leashes usually slung around their necks. The very young dogs and the disobedient ones remained leashed to their owners, who spilled coffee and dropped newspapers every time the pup lurched off after some fun.

I trusted Libro enough to let him go. He'd obeyed in the dog run, come when called. Still no glitches in the software. Besides, I knew he knew I'd saved him and that whatever delinquent desire drove other dogs to run away was eradicated by his wish to keep our relationship together. I unleashed him. He ran off to know and be known by the local population.

He made a friend immediately of a male Portie named Mattie, for Matteus, since he was Portuguese. They chased each other into the underbrush at the base of the park wall, then out again, alternating who was pursuer, who pursued. Libro was having a good leg day. The woman watching Mattie was an English professor. We talked about Queer Theory and medieval studies. A posse approached—a huge young collie named Duncan, a yellow retriever I didn't know, a mutt named Shadow, all with human females by their sides. We suddenly had a pack: five dogs, five women.

"Libro, come!"

"Mattie, come!"

The pack moved off along the path. We passed other packs, stopped, walked some more.

By nine, we'd all been down to Ninety-sixth Street and back. Libro had acquitted himself well in the coming-when-called department. He'd raced in huge circles with Mattie at his heels, wrestled with Shadow, nuzzled Duncan. All the dogs stopped when the young woman with the retriever, a Columbia graduate student, uncorked a water bottle she'd been carrying in her backpack and poured it into her dog's mouth, then into each of four other panting canines who had joined the lineup. Buy a water bottle, I told myself.

Like women at the water well in some ancient village, we shared information. I, the new kid on the block, mostly listened. A man with a collie and a woman with a tiny white dog—the kind I thought of as a pillow with feet—passed, arms around each other, dogs trying to jump between them. Each married to other people, I learned, using dog-walking as a cover. Which led to talk about the man with two spaniels, who was always breaking up and then reconciling with his girlfriend. About the woman with the Akita on a black velvet leash who had lost twenty pounds and recently become a blonde. About the divorced lawyer fighting his wife for custody of their yellow Labrador.

I had little to offer except to recount the things that puzzled me: Libro's limp, his mysterious past, and the upsetting encounter we'd had at Straus Park the week before. The English professor, who had lived all over the world, set me straight, explaining, as to a child, the different status of dogs in other cultures. Her Mexican housekeeper had once repeated a village proverb: I hope when I die that I come back as a dog in an American household. Among Muslims, the professor said, in her best classroom manner, dogs are unclean. The nannies in Straus Park probably came from places where dogs were not pampered household pets, but wild, dirty, feral animals, or, in the poorest places, dinner.

I was thoroughly abashed. I looked at Libro, lying on the ground with his tongue lapping Shadow's face and I tried to imagine another pair of eyes focused on the scene. Cultural context, I told myself. Remember.

EVERY STEP LIBRO TOOK was a clue about the condition of his leg, which changed from one day to the next. A few times, at home, I found him licking his right knee joint and he stopped immediately, as though he'd been caught doing something bad. The people in the dog run said that canines learn to hide their injuries, lest they be cut from the pack. After that, I didn't let on that I'd noticed when he ministered to himself.

Every step was also a clue, I thought, about where he had come from. He had a marked preference for being playful around men, particularly black men, starting with

Clarence, who lived with Lola. Libro followed Clarence around slavishly, nuzzling his leg, asking to be petted, jumping off the ground to land a wet kiss wherever he could. Clarence encouraged him. Lola was not jealous, obsessed as she was with staring down squirrels and birds in the park.

Libro abandoned Clarence only once, hurtling toward a light-skinned man walking two rottweilers. The alarm on the man's face faded when Libro arrived tongue first, ignoring the rottweilers and leaping up to kiss the man. The dogs did mind and were growling menacingly when I arrived, breathless from running, to yank Libro away.

"Do you know him?" I asked the man.

He didn't. Libro kept looking back over his shoulder and up at me, apparently heartbroken.

In the street, he tugged at his leash, tail up, ears flapping, whether the black man who captured his attention was pushing shopping carts full of discarded bottles and cans or wearing Armani and hailing a cab. I learned from the objects of his affection that this behavior was extremely unusual. White people's dogs are generally hostile to black people. Occasionally, I'd hazard further discussion on the admittedly touchy matter. The dogs, I was told by the men Libro pursued, must sense their white owners' fear or caution. But Libro, I knew, was act-ing out his own agenda, not mine. In the mystery of his past, he'd known, loved, and probably lived with a black man, I was sure.

We started walking at night with Lola and Clarence. I plied Clarence, a doctor, for information about Libro's limp, his runny nose, his diet. One week, Lola had a silver chain around her neck. Then she had a flashing red light on her collar, so Clarence could see her in the dark. Her movements became a blip on a radar screen. A few days later, she had a ball that glowed in the nighttime grass, special order from an exclusive catalog. Libro and I were either the poor relations or the pure ones, I wasn't sure.

Somehow, I'd gotten the idea that I didn't want to spoil Libro. He wouldn't get a treat every time he sat down and he wouldn't have a laundry hamper full of toys. He didn't need a wardrobe. We'd be propless, just he and I, interrogating, as the postmodernists say, the question of living together.

Other nights, we wandered alone along Riverside Drive past green wooden benches turned into love seats. If a couple was embracing and kissing, as many were, Libro would pull on his leash and try to stick his wet nose between them, not to pry them apart, but to participate in the affection. Most couples were good-natured enough to laugh.

We went together into unknown territory, down into the park or along the Drive some two or three miles, up to Grant's Tomb, places I, a street-smart New York female, avoided after dark. But I had now not only a companion, but a protector. In spite of his marshmallow character, some people thought Libro was a pit bull, others just that he was a dog you don't mess with. I felt safe. And because I felt safe, I felt free.

I sang "When the Saints Go Marching In." I skipped. When he raced ahead of me, I kept up, singing "Lullaby of Broadway" and then "Camptown Ladies," trying to clap the chorus—"oh doo da doo"—with the leash handle in my hand. Maybe, I thought, people had dogs in their lives because it allowed them to do silly things like skip and sing along the street without censure. "It's not me; it's my dog."

I yanked him away from chicken bones on the ground. Slowing the pace, I hummed "We Shall Overcome" and he slowed down. There may be nothing that makes a person feel in sync with the world quite as much as walking along with a canine in step beside you.

WEEKEND NIGHTS, RIVERSIDE PARK and the Drive became a part of Havana, Trinidad, or Port-au-Prince. Cars were parked with their doors open and radios blaring steel guitars or trumpets, sometimes a baseball game. Inside the park, clans gathered, teenaged boys playing soccer and dressed up girls looking on shyly, twirling their hair, the women cooking over portable barbecues or unpacking large aluminum pots of food, the men playing cards. After sunset, you could hear the beat of the music from portable radios or the occasional live singer with a guitar blocks away.

Once, when Libro and I ambled up to the picnicking Latinos, I had to hold the leash tight against the lure of the food. A little dark-haired girl in a pink dress toddled over and reached out to touch him. He greeted her, which is to say, in spite of his leash but because of my inexperience, he jumped up to lick her face. The girl fell, blubbering. Libro looked alarmed and made as if to comfort her, while two men in dark pants and white shirts came rushing toward us.

"*Siéntate*, Libro!"

He looked from the fallen girl to me.

"*Siéntate*, Libro. Now!"

He sat just as one of the men scooped the little girl into his arms.

"*El perro habla español?*"

Yes, I said, the dog spoke Spanish.

We were sorry, in English. Libro started to get up, but thought better of it. Another *siéntate* didn't hurt.

"*Se llama* Libro."

The men laughed and the girl's tears slowed. Two boys on roller blades joined us. I said how intellectual Libro was, how studious. Calling a dog *Libro* is pretty funny in Spanish.

"*El perro es tu amigo,*" the man said to the girl. The dog is your friend. And she reached down from the safety of her father's arms to touch my pal, while I held his exuberance down.

"Good boy."

"*Muy bien.*"

Biscuits galore, kiddo, you've averted an incident.

The boys on roller blades laughed. Enrique and Paco, their names were. Their parents were cousins, born in the Dominican Republic, and the boys were eleven and twelve, bicultural and bilingual, wearing Nike sneakers, Tommy Hilfinger T-shirts, and Gap jeans. They wanted to know in English if they could play with Libro. I said they should ask him.

Enrique was younger and bolder. He skated away, calling for Libro to follow. Libro did, dragging his leash. Enrique stopped. Libro jumped, stumpy tail wagging, front paws in the air, and landed a kiss on the boy's face. Enrique laughed and glided off again. They disappeared into the darkness and when they came back, Enrique had hold of Libro's leash and was trying to get him to play husky.

"Pull," he was shouting, "*tira*, Libro."

Libro smiled and pulled.

THE ENCAMPMENT OF HOMELESS men along the drive near 108th Street had always seemed full of potential menace, but Libro's presence made it less so. He'd made a particular friend of a young handsome dreadlocked fellow named Cedric, who spoke with elegant diction and, unlike some of his friends, looked directly at me. I came to think of him as he thought of himself, a fallen prince of the West Indies.

Every once in a while, a woman appeared among Cedric's crew, but the women didn't stay long. I had the impression they weren't welcome. Libro, however, sometimes spread his attention around.

He wagged his tail at a woman who leaned against the stone park wall, some distance from where Cedric and the others had spread their cardboards on the benches and secured their full shopping carts for the night. She was in her thirties, barefoot, with a turban on her head.

"Hey there," she said to him.

I let him go and he embraced her, with high speed sloppy kisses and a firm hug.

"Oh baby baby baby," she said, arms tight around him. "Gimmee a kiss, baby." He stood up on his hind legs, which he hardly ever did. "I ain't had no lovin' like this in a year," she said.

He obliged. It was hard to tear him away, but a few yards along was the shape of a body under a layer of clothes asleep on a bench. Libro raced over and stood still, staring, then went up and nudged the sleeping face, very gently. The man bolted up with a howl. I was prepared to run.

"I'm so sorry."

"Yo! Pooch!"

"I'm really very sorry."

The man was rubbing Libro's head.

"I think he was checking to see that you're not dead."

"Yeah, well, okay pooch, I'm not dead yet."

"Libro! Come!"

Before we turned away from the park, we passed a man in a wheelchair holding a hypodermic in his right hand, about to thrust it into his strapped-up left arm. Libro stopped. He and the man stared at each other, not the way Libro played chicken with squirrels, more a what's-going-on-here eyeballing. The man lowered his right hand. Libro moved forward and stopped to be petted.

"I'm sorry you had to see that, boy," the man said.

Bad Mom

....

Mostly, my work consists of staring at a computer screen, swiveling in my blue chair, stretching, tapping some keys on the keyboard, pulling pages out of the printer, reading, shredding, putting my hands on the keyboard, and staring some more. Part of the fantasy of bringing Libro home, I'm sure, was of myself at work (tweed jacket, leather elbow patches) with him snoozing peacefully at my feet.

Snoozing was the last thing on his mind. He liked to stand in the leg space under my desk and box me with his paw. Sometimes, he just wanted to hold hands. Mostly, he wanted to climb into my lap, stare at the computer screen, and put his paws on the keyboard. I kept losing track of sentences because halfway through, I'd stop to say *off* or *down* and forget where I was headed. When I got up to make coffee, he followed. When I tried to read with a critical eye, looking for *off* and *down* to pop up like grinning Cheshire cats in the forest of my prose, he tried to climb all over me or cover the pages with his paws.

This would not do. If I didn't work, he wouldn't have biscuits. My explanation fell on deaf floppy ears. If I couldn't write, I'd get unbalanced and probably go insane. He didn't care. Off. Down. Leave me alone. Go away. He didn't care. Deep in those amber eyes, I saw a threat.

I carried an ancient, irrational, gender-specific paranoia: Men don't respect my work! I'm supposed to be doing meatballs and mending. I should sew. It was crazy, even in human terms. My father had supported my writing since childhood, bringing notebooks and pens home from the candy store he owned. Peter had been head of the fan club.

Big burden for a little dog. I told Libro I was sorry and offered a trade. He could have the couch if he let me work at my desk. No more off or down. Knock yourself out. He took the couch and that was the end of the problem. The air conditioner hummed away and he snoozed or investigated parts of his body while I put my hands on the keyboard and stared at the screen.

I had a bit of a life away from the keyboard and the dog. I even left the house at times, without him. Dressed in clothes he couldn't jump on, perfumed and adorned with makeup, I'd lean over to kiss him good-bye, check that he had fresh water. He'd reproach me with his beautiful eyes. Libro did pathetic better than any person I knew, myself included. It worked. I felt like Joan Crawford in a 1940s movie. Bad mom.

BY JULY, MY ASSUMPTIONS about dogs and the people who loved them had begun to crumble. Canine-assisted living was clearly not confined to California. I was liking Libro even more than I had Ariel. The freedom to leave for Paris on a moment's notice, I was starting to think, was perhaps not the epitome of what life had to offer. I'd lost my aversion to dirty paws, blubbery mouths, even shenanigans near the jogging track.

Last to fall were a set of inchoate 1950s ideas about Mom, Dad, Dick, Jane, and Spot. There were some conventional nuclear families with pets in my neighborhood, but not very many. Most domestic arrangements were distinctly modern—single women, single men with dogs, divorced people sharing custody, and lesbian or gay couples. It took me awhile to catch on.

When Mattie, the Porty, appeared in the park with a slim blond woman instead of the English professor, I actually thought she might be a walker, but of course she wasn't. She was a writer. Mattie actually had two mommies. Many dogs had two daddies. Nobody seemed any the worse for any of it. In the big scheme of things, the dog world was far less bigoted than the civilization that surrounded it.

I WAS FEELING EASIER ABOUT leaving Libro alone. He knew the rules. He had his couch. I went out to have coffee with a friend at the café on the corner. I came back to a peaceful pup with a wagging tail and sloppy welcoming kisses that sent my dry cleaning bill skyrocketing. I went to dinner, to movies, to the theater, all without him and with increasing confidence that home sweet home would not be befouled or shredded in my absence. I trusted him, although I suspected that he understood he was on probation and that if he ever felt entirely safe and settled in, I might expect less perfect behavior.

The ritual remained the same: pathos on my departure, joy at my return. No resentment. That was the oddest thing of all. When I'd been left alone and pathetic, believe me, I'd never have wagged my tail if the leaver returned. Not even ten years later. I carried my scars like tattoos, my grudges as permanent as my name. Not Libro. For him, apparently, they were watercolor; they washed off.

It became routine. I went out. I came back. But one day, he wasn't on the couch. He wasn't lying on the rug or slurping at his water bowl. I found him in the bathroom, his punishment spot, with his head hanging down. A self-punishing dog! What a marvel! But what had he done? I looked around. No urine trickle anywhere, no smelly brown piles on the floor, no torn newspapers—all minor transgressions dating from our earliest days together.

Then I saw my datebook on the floor. It was a small red leather-covered book, English made, with a pale blue page for each day. I had last seen it on the desk. I picked it up and a big handful of pages fell out, saliva stained and ragged at the edges. The summer months were missing.

I wheeled around. He knew. How could he not know? Libro was still punishing himself.

My life was in that book. Deadlines. Appointments with editors. Dinners with friends. Gynecology check-ups. Lectures and seminars coming up in the fall. Birthdays. Concerts. Readings. Tennis. A day with my brother at the beach. A trip with Susan to the Alice Austen house in Staten Island. A walk, a drive, a movie.

"Bad dog!" I screamed.

He didn't look up.

I tried to stick the torn pages under his nose, but he wouldn't raise his head.

I kicked him. Hard. In the ribs. He ran for cover under the sink. My nails cut into the palms of my fisted hands. He cowered, like a turtle trying to pull into its shell, and then he ran into my study.

I'm not much of a believer in divine intervention, but something bigger and better than my enraged self led me to the hallway door, got it open, and called Libro. He hesitated, cringing, looked at me in terror and with reproach, and then rushed out into the hallway in a pumpernickel blur. I slammed the door and paced, heart thumping, gasping for air, until reason finally returned. I couldn't think of anyone to call.

It was the most abject apology I've ever made. Still shaking, I found him huddled in the stairwell. He didn't run. He knew it was over. I knelt beside him and he kissed my face, frantically. We went back upstairs and I fed him biscuits and then we went out. I was crying.

My neighbor Lisa was walking Baxter just as we reached the street. I blurted a horrified account of what had happened. She put her arm around me and Baxter barked. Libro tried to get between us.

"Down. Off."

Lisa said if I ever felt that way again, I should bring Libro to her place.

In the park, others said they too had lost their tempers.

The line that separates me from "them"—a decent person from an abuser, a citizen from a perp, a human from a dog—was turning out to be less a line than an undulating gauze fence, full of holes. The dog people understood bad behavior as temporary. I didn't.

He chewed my little red book, Josie's wise owner said, not because he wanted to keep me home with him, away from any appointments, but because he missed me. It was, Dorothy the dog walker added, the object in my office most doused with my smell, the thing I touched all day long. He ate me because he loved me. Ah!

I watched Libro at the other end of the dusty dog run, trying to get Amber to give up her ball and pay attention to him. He boxed her side. He licked her face.

"Libro, come!"

I knelt in the dirt, hugging him with one arm and scratching behind his ear with the other. He looked away. Then he looked directly into my eyes and licked my face—my cheeks, my forehead, and my mouth. He rolled over. I rubbed his belly. His legs kicked with glee. I forgave myself.

ALTHOUGH I DIDN'T THINK so at the time, it seems, in retrospect, that I let him into my bed because I felt guilty about my cruelty. All I thought then was that the walls I had erected against intimacy were arbitrary. Lots of people slept with their dogs. What was my problem?

Sex, partly. Maybe entirely. Since Peter's departure, I'd reverted to a kind of virginity in decor, with antique embroidered pillowcases, white sheets, and a pale seersucker quilt. Not exactly canine-friendly. So the idea of Libro in my bed was unthinkable from a Martha Stewart point of view, at first.

In the weeks after he came to live with me, hungrily trading information with the dog people in the park, I had discovered all kinds of sleeping arrangements—on the bed, at the side or foot of the bed, far away—along with a certain defensiveness on my part.

"Does he sleep with you?" a woman asked.

"Oh no, I'm afraid."

"Why? He won't hurt you."

"I'm not afraid of him. It's me. I'm worried about what *I* might do."

The woman looked horrified and backed away.

When I told the story to friends, I embellished: "It's not because he's a dog that I worry. It's because he's so young. I wouldn't want to add another kind of child abuse to what he's already endured." I wish I'd actually said that.

Having no experience with canine ardor, I couldn't quite name the feelings I had in relation to his body.

Fear had been first, then timidity, based on how strange it all seemed. His tail wagged when he was happy or about to be fed, but also when I accidentally stepped on his paw. His ears flopped, twitched, or rose according to no pattern I could discern. But he'd been showing me how his body worked. Patting him atop his head, the way people do in cartoons, made him flinch, so I understood that the raised hand was a threat and never did it. He liked being rubbed and gently scratched behind his ears, under his chin, down his spine, on his rump.

He began asking for what he wanted by boxing my leg.

He boxed.

"What?" I asked.

He stood at the door.

Out.

Or he stood at his food bowl.

Nourishment.

Or he lay down on the bathroom tile and stretched his legs toward me, the expression on his face hopeful.

Massage.

Massages for his bad leg were now part of our daily ritual. I moved two fingers slowly down his spine, relaxing it. Sometimes he sighed. With both hands, I gently kneaded each knee joint and the tendons stretching to his feet.

Occasionally, I gave him a doggy reflexology treatment. I did for him what I would have wanted done for me and it must have been the right thing, for Libro took to coming up to me while I was working, boxing my leg, getting me to follow him, and asking for more massage.

Since Peter's departure, I'd gradually relearned what I once knew—to have a life of my own. I had even, painfully, made peace with eating meals alone. But I missed the constant talk and touch of daily life with another person. Is it time to do the laundry? Now, where did I put my glasses? Want to go to the park and watch the sunset? Touch was the glue. The quick hug, the cursory kiss, the toes touching in sleep.

Now I had both, in a form I'd never imagined. I talked to Libro. He answered, in his way, whimpering, croaking, yelping, dancing around, or turning his head away. He still hadn't helped find misplaced glasses. When I touched him, almost always, he touched back—paws around my shoulders, tongue on my neck, crawling beside or on top of me if I lay on the couch reading the newspaper, cuddling in my armpit.

The biggest night of our lives so far began with us on the living room couch, watching the eleven o'clock news. While the sports report was on, instead of leading Libro away to my writing studio and his fluffy bed, I simply changed into my nightgown and brushed my teeth. Libro jumped off the couch and followed me, watching the clothes-changing and toothbrushing with what I thought was wonder.

I went into the bedroom, got into bed, turned the reading light on, and pulled up the covers. He apparently couldn't believe the forbidden territory was suddenly okay. He approached tentatively, first a chin at the bed's edge, eyes questioning, then a hoist, front legs up, a lift, back legs up. All of him stood on the seersucker quilt, asking, What now? I let him lie beside me and turned out the light.

He snuggled closer, back against me. I put an arm across his shoulders and drifted away, only to be startled awake by a deep bass snore, then a wheeze, then another. I did what I would do with any male, turned him over. He licked my face. I drifted away, accommodating the snoring, but an acrid smell yanked me awake again. Peter would sometimes crawl into bed after I was asleep, reeking of beer, but this was a smell more sour, more scatological. I willed myself asleep. I woke. He licked. He wheezed. He farted. He got up and shook his body. The metal tags hanging from his collar clanked me awake again. He lay down and then got up.

When he stepped on me, it was over. I loved him, but I also loved a good night's sleep. He let me take him to his own bed in my study as though he'd known all along that it was his real place. We never spoke of what had happened.

Hot Town, Summer in the City

....

As August came and summer wore on, I began to feel trapped with Libro in our urban paradise. During the hottest afternoons, our tar beach—the small, asphalt-floored terrace outside my writing studio—steamed, even with the green and white striped umbrella casting shade. The containers of rosemary and basil, clematis and columbine, lemon-scented geraniums needed watering twice a day. I could bear no more than an hour outdoors, Libro even less. He retreated inside to lie, panting, near the air conditioner or the floor fan. The racing engine that was his heart and lungs scared me.

He should swim, I thought. He should cool off and paddle around and so should I, but the city offered no venue for joint aquatics. Josie, who was, after all, a Portuguese water dog, was being driven to a pool in Connecticut, where she could splash around with other Porties, a kind of country club to which no boxers were invited. I went to the health club. Libro got showered with hoses when the supers on the street washed down the sidewalks, like any urban urchin. We'd walked at the edge of the Hudson River and I'd eyed the murky currents, although Libro was more interested in the condoms and picnic debris that lay along the ground.

On a desolate stretch at the river's edge one afternoon, I made the decision for him. Far from the men fishing for catfish and away from the couples embracing on blankets, we climbed out about three feet on some slimy rocks—he more agile and surefooted than I—and sat down. I urged him in. He didn't know what I was talking about. Naturally, I thought, he's a city dog, he knows sidewalks, traffic, cafés, grocery stores, pet stores, even bookstores—we'd been browsing in local bookstores, where I'd explained, effectively enough, that his name was Libro and he had an affinity for the products they sold—but a river wasn't in his repertory.

Still holding his leash, I gave him a little nudge. He

sniffed the wet rocks and went forward, nose to the ground and then nose to the river and then nose in the river. His head went under, his ears, his neck, then his shoulders. His stumpy tail waved in the air and I stood, poised to jump in to save him. Could I chest-carry a soggy boxer?

He didn't need me. Up came his head, finally, with a "what the hell was that?" expression on his face. He paddled briefly and then he was up on the rocks, shaking the sludgy water all over me. I'd probably made him sick.

I watched him guiltily the rest of the day, awaiting signs of intestinal upset or plague, but Libro was fine. I was feeling more and more trapped. Other summers, I'd escaped to rented seaside houses or, with Peter, to California, but the roller-coaster finances of a writer's life had dipped and I'd taken in recent years to depending on the kindness of friends.

Libro made a difference. Lacking a car or the funds to have him crated up and shipped air freight, without martinis, movies, or recycled air vents to keep him comfortable, I was stuck. The Long Island Railroad's policy was that dogs were okay—"just bring him in his cage," the woman on the phone said. Right. Maybe I'd been able to lift him the day I brought him home—not now. Months of brown pellets masquerading as lamb and rice had an effect. The air was back in him. His ribs were less sunken, his legs longer, his chest no longer concave. He was bigger. We were stuck in the city.

My friends, all of whom would have to accommodate Libro one way or another, had already endured many kinds of transgressions on my part. I owed some of them money. I disagreed with a few over political matters — although my tendency on encountering such differences usually led me to walk away righteous and muttering. I'd lost two friends, decades apart, when romantic obsession over two different men simply wore down the shoulders I cried on. My women friends had little truck with suffering over men and neither did I, except when it came to me. On the whole, they were a loyal lot and I was a friend worth having and we'd all been building these connections for a long time, so it would take an earthquake to rend them asunder.

Libro was the earthquake, albeit a minor one, in relationships that had withstood questionable boyfriends, career success and failure, divorces and deaths. To my astonishment, forgetting that I had until very recently been one myself, I actually knew people who were afraid of or just didn't like dogs and didn't want "them" in their cars or their houses. Some considered "them" a nuisance, others loved dogs but had husbands/boyfriends/girlfriends/

mothers-in-law who didn't. A few said they were allergic, but I didn't believe them. Libro wasn't "them," he was Libro. The distinction fell on deaf ears.

When Wendy invited us to Sag Harbor, then, I was relieved. When she said he would have to sleep outside, I began to snarl like an animal rights activist. I was well on my way to developing a screwy, dangerous moral code: People who liked dogs and Libro were good; people who didn't were bad. I could see my Rolodex shrinking.

But the truth, as always, was more complicated. Diana was a wonderful friend to me, marveling at my accounts of every amazing thing the dog did and listening with patience and without judgment to the saga of my deepening crush on him. She offered intuitive advice—she was, after all, a good therapist. In response to my shyness and uncertainty about Libro's body, she'd said, "If you find yourself touching him and going into a fugue state, call me. Right away." So far, I hadn't needed to.

She did those things, however, on the telephone. Face-to-face, in Libro's presence, she recoiled, feigning allergies, but ultimately confessing to fear and dislike. Not of him, but of the canine "them." She claimed to have been mauled to death by a vicious dog in another life and who was I to question that? I wouldn't have to lock him in the bathroom when she came to visit, but I would have to insist he stay away from her.

Before she and her husband Stephen came for their first dinner after Libro moved in, I explained Diana's attitude to Libro. He watched me light the charcoal grill on the terrace and set the table, tail wagging, knowing something big was up. The bell rang. He raced to the door.

I must have said *off* and *down* a hundred times that evening. Our guests brought a box of doggy junk food treats for Libro and a fine wine for us. While I served the wine and turned the sizzling chicken on the grill, Stephen gamely tussled with him, but Diana huddled into herself. Libro kept trying to win her over. Every rebuff provoked more kisses. He sat at her feet with that doleful expression calculated to make anyone feel guilty. She didn't respond. She was a therapist and couldn't be baited.

When the food was on the table, Libro was banished into the apartment. He didn't go gently. In fact, he sat in the doorway doing what I would come to call his Dachau dog act, his eyes huge and pleading, his cheeks sinking more deeply into his little face, his body shriveling, a fine and moving imitation of a concentration camp inmate. Stephen fell for it and wanted to feed him chicken. Diana tried to get us to talk about other things.

• • •

WE MADE DO, THROUGH increasingly humid days and nights, round-the-clock air-conditioning and walks that consisted of little more than a descent to the street and a plop onto the concrete sidewalk. Libro was unable to walk more than a few steps in the torpid air and I stood over him, begging him to move. Eventually, I just sat on the sidewalk beside him 'til he was ready to go on.

Ted and Sophia, on the third floor, had gone to London for the summer, a perk of living on an academic's schedule. No lasagna scents enticed Libro's nose to their door. Charles, who lived next door to them, went to a beach house for long weekends, and since he left at dawn for Wall Street during the week, we never saw him. Even the boys next door were sparse, out working at summer jobs or looking for summer jobs or roller-blading into the night, as our encounters on the staircase revealed. If I'd had an analyst, she would have been out of town.

The people and their dogs in the park scattered too. The morning posses were half as large as they had been and the dog run at midday was an arid desert. Josie went to the country. Mattie went to day care while the women he lived with went to Europe. Lola was entering show events and Clarence was shopping at Ralph Lauren for the clothes to wear to those events. Every once in a while, we saw Lola in the park, practicing, standing perfectly still, squared off. Libro walked back and forth, right in front of her, and she didn't blink. He sighed and walked away.

ROSEMARY SAVED US. We had been friends since we were girl poets together in the heady days of the seventies, the last time I felt part of any stable community. Now we were grown women with books under our belts, lovers come and gone, each, for now, living alone—I in the city, she in the country—with dogs.

We had a country weekend planned, at last. For his first overnight, Libro inherited my green and white canvas beach bag. Not knowing what kind of traveler he might be, I packed bowls, food, comforter, and a half-chewed teddy bear. We brought Rosemary a straw angel to hang in her office and Rags, her dog, a rawhide bone. There were probably stores on Madison Avenue specializing in hostess gifts for dogs, but we were determinedly not of the Gucci canine set.

That morning, before we left, I sat him down and explained the rules about being a houseguest. No peeing on the floor. No jumping on furniture. No dashing off in the middle of the night because you're homesick or can't tolerate being on someone else's turf for a few days. Help with the dishes and bring a gift. Be good. We want to be invited back. He listened seriously, head cocked.

When Rosemary arrived to pick us up, Libro clambered into the back seat of her navy blue Volkswagon, which was covered with a blanket and clumps of shedded hair belonging to Rags, the nine-year-old Belgian sheepdog, who awaited us in the country. Like Libro, Rags was adopted, but she was a planned-for dog, decided-on, searched-for, and chosen at a local rescue society soon after Rosemary moved out of Manhattan. Our dogs had met when Rosemary stayed in town for a week, a pleasant but uneventful encounter, but Libro had never spent a weekend with her.

As we drove north, his stumpy tail whirled so fast he might have mixed cake batter with it. He tried to sit on my lap, to watch the road through the front window, to drive, to lick Rosemary's face in gratitude. With the authority born of having lived with a dog for some time, she sent him to the backseat again, where he stood up, sat down, licked the windows, stared at the passing scenery. Pure joy.

And what would he do, I wondered, in nature? Had he ever seen a stream or field, much less a deer? I counted on Rags to show him the ropes.

What Libro did in the country was just be a dog. A good dog, but a dog nonetheless. Soon after we arrived, while Rosemary unloaded the car, we explored. As we crossed the stream near Rosemary's saltbox house to

climb the hill beyond, Rags sat down in the stream, letting the water delight her. Libro was more cautious, step-
ping gingerly from stone to stone, looking back at Rags as
though he couldn't understand what she was doing. She
charged to the right up the hill, he bounded off to the
left. I let him go. We all met up in a meadow and again
near a pond. I lay down in the sun. Libro licked my face,
but then he was gone, chasing after rustling sounds in the
trees as though he'd been there all his life.

The dogs ate on the back porch, separately. Rosemary
and I went out to a restaurant. Later, I made him a pallet
on the floor of the screened-in porch near Rags, who was
relaxing and looking only mildly interested on her bed.
He fell into a deep, aired-out country sleep and I went
upstairs, where I did the same until I heard paws clicking
on the wooden-floored hallway.

Rosemary's house is small but complicated, with a
twisting staircase to the second story and a warren of
rooms, a layout utterly unlike the bland architectural ra-
tionality of our city home. But he found me. I pointed to
a braided rug at the foot of the bed and told him to lie
down, which he did. If he snored, I didn't hear it.

The dogs went their separate ways, inhabiting the
same space without much recognition or interaction.
Rags had her spots, she knew the turf and the routine.

Libro was on vacation. He deferred to Rosemary in the house, did as he was told, and learned to let himself out the back door, a relief, I imagine, from having to ask a human to trot down four flights of stairs with him.

There was a solitary independence about Rags and other country dogs I'd seen that I couldn't imagine Libro possessing, even as he got older and farther from the trauma that had brought him into my life. He ran off into the woods with gusto, but returned frequently, climbing into my lap as I sat reading outdoors, getting Rosemary to let him into the house, and then pushing the door to get out. He was clearly the product of city streets, dog runs, packs of park-strolling people and canines. He'd made me think of my grandma, who'd lived in city bustle all her life, taking in the world on the benches of the Grand Concourse in the Bronx and then, later, the veranda of a South Beach, Miami, residence hotel, before the developers came. When she visited my parents, in their quiet condo on a canal, she was bored.

Saturday afternoon, when I grew restless at Rosemary's house, I decided to go for a short walk down to the large river nearby, maybe swim, maybe see if Libro would too. My friend was deep in a chapter of her new book, but she directed me—along the paved road to the break in the fence on the other side, down, bearing right to a meadow, then around a thicket of birches. . . . I grew glassy-eyed. She drew a map. I was still glassy-eyed. I can tell you the fastest way from the upper west side to the lower east side of Manhattan by subway, using three different train lines and a secret underground passageway, but fences, meadows, and thickets as landmarks elude me. I'm not even sure of the difference between a meadow and a field.

Well, Rags knew the way, Rosemary assured me, and so I folded the map into my pocket, got Libro's leash and Rags's too, and set off. Dogs in front and moving fast, we hugged the shoulder of the road, then crossed it, but no interrupted fence made itself known to me or to Rags either. After half a mile, I knew we'd gone too far and turned back, watching Rags for clues.

"Find the river," I said.

A brief turn of her head and I presumed she'd obeyed. We squeezed through a hole in the fence and descended a path that got more and more overgrown the farther we got from the road. Bees, wasps, butterflies, mosquitoes, dragonflies, and other airborne things I couldn't identify flew around; Libro tried to catch them in his mouth. I considered letting the dogs off their leashes, but feared they'd get lost. Or I'd get lost.

Rags plodded along matter-of-factly, like someone on the way to pick up dry cleaning or a newspaper, but Libro

was in his own private Coney Island, fascinated by everything he'd never seen before, which was everything. He
stopped at fallen trees, peed on high weeds, barreled
through bushes so prickly I had to hold them aside so
that I could pass. I worried about ticks. We came to a
meadow or a field. He tried to chase something moving
at the other end—a rabbit, perhaps, or a bear—and I
wrenched my shoulder holding him back.

I told the dogs to sit and I sat too, checking the ground
for snakes first, then listening for the sound of the river.
Silence. I looked up at the afternoon sun, to get a bearing. It was sinking, but that told me nothing about the
river. I felt uneasy. Libro lay down and only then did I remember his gimpy leg and feel sorry about this forced
march. I tried to tell from Rags's face whether we were in
a familiar place, but she was blank—accommodating,
but blank.

I stood. The dogs got up. We were lost. I wasn't sure
where we'd entered the meadow or how to get out of it. I
slacked Rags's leash, that she might lead us to safety. She
looked to me for direction.

In the end, we did find our way back, although I had
a few Indiana Jones moments doing so, hacking my
way through brambles and branches and afraid of all
living things that dwell in nature, except for the two

dogs and myself. On safe ground again, Libro rushed for the water bowl on the back porch; Rags went off to a secret hiding spot. I, tail between my legs, told Rosemary we hadn't found the river. We'd been gone no more than half an hour.

ON SUNDAY AFTERNOON, Rosemary drove us to the train station. This was a little risky. Dogs were prohibited on most rail lines, but this particular one was reportedly more lenient. When I'd called to check, the stationmaster said it was up to the conductor. Libro, I'd told him, just be as charming as you can be. As always.

Rosemary waited until the train pulled in, kissed me good-bye, and let Libro lick her face. She would stay in her car until we'd left the station, lest Libro and I find ourselves booted onto the tracks.

We boarded. Libro went down the aisle, sniffing each row and eventually choosing one midway down the mostly empty car, on the Hudson River side. A few passengers looked amused. A mother in one row drew her young daughter closer. As naturally as any commuter, Libro climbed onto a green leather seat, sat on his haunches, and turned his face to the grimy window. The river sparkled through the smudges.

"Is that a dog?"

The conductor stood there, ticket punch in hand.

Uh oh. I imagined us out on the road, hitchhiking.

"I'm not sure."

As, indeed, I wasn't. Oh yes, he had floppy ears and paws and a snout and a propensity to lick faces, but if you'd seen him riding the train, serenely studying the passing scenery, you would wonder too.

The dog had to ride on the floor, the conductor said, and so the dog did. I paid my fare. I was a woman traveling with a dog. Her dog. For better or for worse, I had a dog.

Cool

A Star Is Born

....

I kept none of what was happening to myself. I talked ad nauseam to anyone with a dog who would talk to me. Does yours limp? How much do you feed her? Where does he sleep? Feel Libro's nose — would you call that wet and cold? It seemed to me that *wet* and *cold* were relative, subjective terms, like *wind chill*, which describes the "feel" of cold on the skin, but whose skin, I always wanted to ask?

Rosemary, who is five years younger than I am but has lived with her dog for nine years, acted like a know-it-all big sister. "Don't feed him from the table," she said. I didn't. "Keep him off the furniture," she said. I didn't.

Diana mercifully restrained herself from analyzing my relationship with Libro. My old friend Timothy, who lives in Boston, wasn't so lucky; when he adopted a dog, the people in his therapy group said he was just avoiding his intimacy-with-women problems. I would have choked them.

In chronic wonder, amusement, and chagrin, I told stories about Libro to my father, who just grunted, to my brother, who responded with stories of his own, and to friends near and far, on the telephone, via e-mail, to friends who got it and even to those who didn't. It is no surprise, then, given my profession, that I wrote about him.

It was a short essay about how I'd brought him home from the park and found myself no longer living alone. A magazine editor liked it and sent a photographer, who arrived loaded with cameras at eight o'clock on a sunny morning, accompanied by her male assistant carrying shields, filters, changing bags, and film, and a spiffy, punky young woman in black to do my hair and make-up. Bathed and brushed, Libro was going to have to face the lens au naturel.

He was so nervous he had an accident on the kitchen floor. It was, after all, his first media appearance. I thought the photographer would take the time to bond with Libro, put him at ease, get some rapport with her subject, but no, she and her assistant immediately started looking at light.

I had a few ideas. My terrace was lush with twining blue morning glories on a white fence, delicate bleeding heart ferns in terra-cotta, gorgeous geraniums in cobalt blue planters. A photograph there would, perhaps, make an ironic point about nature in the city. No, she said, the sunlight was way too harsh. What then, I offered, about the elaborate marble fountain in Straus Park, the nice contrast of the dark dog clambering around in it? She wasn't impressed. The sliding pond in the children's playground, down on the drive, a comical Libro poised and posed at the top, eager to descend? This was something he'd discovered on his own. Far be it for me to encourage stupid pet tricks. When Libro climbed and slid —sometimes taking off before he reached the bottom, so he would land in the sandbox—passersby stopped to laugh. The photographer looked at me like I must be kidding.

All this time, a cleaned up Libro was trying to make friends with the new people in our space—sniffing their legs, sitting down for them—and getting nowhere. The photographer and her assistant decided to scout the light in the neighborhood and while they were gone, Libro sat on my lap as the hot curlers came out and tried to lick my face while foundation was being spread on it.

In the end, photography really is about the light and my instinct for narrative is not. We all trooped out to the park. I sat where the photographer liked the light—in an open grass field, under a tree, on a bench. Libro's attitude was far better than mine. He sat. He lay down. He looked toward the camera. He stayed. He was having fun. I was beginning to get big ideas about his future.

The increasing heat caused rivulets of sweat in my makeup, down my neck, and all over my silk-swathed upper body. It also caused Libro to pant a lot, his enormous tongue drooping like a pink bib down the front of his face and neck. Put your tongue back in your mouth for the picture, I thought, bossy as any stage mother. He couldn't.

The neighborhood is accustomed to cameras and entourages. The television show *Law and Order* often sets up on one of the side streets and we get a lot of movie people, their huge trucks taking up all available parking spaces and their daily sidewalk buffets enticing the passing dogs. We've had artificial rain machines turn blissful evenings into miserable downpours and klieg lights turn the dead of night into high noon. Not to mention the stars who live nearby and wander around without causing much stir.

So nobody paid attention to the four of us—photographer, assistant, sweaty me, and happy Libro

—the makeup person having left for her day job at a salon and having found me a lost cause anyway. While we were positioned half in shade and half in sunlight under a big elm, the assistant juggling the light shield, which looked like a huge diaphragm, first on our left, then on our right, a man and dog stopped to watch. He was a tall, lanky man, the kind my grandma called a long drink of water, and the dog was a dachshund, who looked like the man, just turned ninety degrees. I thought there was a funny symmetry about the tall man with the little dog and the rather petite me with the big panting canine, but didn't have much time to pursue the thought because Libro kept turning his head to look at them, nearly ruining the shot. The assistant was dispatched to ask them to leave. The man waved and walked away.

By sunset, the photographer had shot a dozen rolls of film. I was afraid the pictures would be banal. Libro, rewarded at home with a handful of biscuits and a big dish of food, went immediately to sleep.

IN SEPTEMBER, THE DOGS came back to the park, like swallows to Capistrano. Back from the Vineyard, the Berkshires, the Hamptons, and doggy day care. The morning cliques and posses came apart and regrouped. Dogs I had never seen before appeared, like a young female boxer who caught Libro's eye, but was not allowed to stop by the man and woman jogging with her. She looked longingly back over her shoulder that morning and from then on, but she kept on jogging. The man with the spaniels, who had accompanied us to the pet store, showed up again after a summer in San Francisco. He and the woman he lived with had decided to separate, but couldn't agree on how to divide the dogs.

On the way home, Libro met his first enemy. There'd been growling in the park and an occasional dogfight, but Libro had always remained aloof. I couldn't say then and can't say now what happened when he saw the shaggy auburn dog crossing the street, walking placidly unleashed beside a man who was talking on his cell phone. It wasn't pretty.

Libro growled, a deep, continuous sound like a huge diesel truck engine churning. I told him to stop. He pulled hard on his leash and the other dog looked back while the man kept talking on his phone. We were on the sidewalk now, several feet behind them and Libro was pulling harder. Eager to play, I thought.

"Don't worry," I always said, in similar situations, "he's absolutely friendly." But the man ahead didn't look up or back at me and so I said it to myself. Libro's friendly. Still, I restrained him.

He wasn't playing and in that moment, he wasn't friendly. As we came near, Libro broke away from me and leaped on the auburn dog, who fought back. Terrified by the blur of paws, teeth, and fur, and the racket of snarls, I nonetheless reached into the maelstrom, grabbing for Libro's leash or collar. I failed, but the man with the phone managed to pull him off.

"Lie down," I said. "Bad dog." He was still growling. What I wanted to do was cuddle him, for Libro looked as terrified as I felt.

"You've got to control your dog," the man said, flipping his cell phone closed and bending to inspect his, who was panting.

The other dog wasn't hurt at all, but Libro had a deep bite behind his ear. Blood ran down the side of his face. I know compassion was called for but, in truth, what I felt was shame. Somewhere in the murk of not knowing what it was to be a woman living with a dog, and in spite of all denials, I thought I was raising a New Age non-aggressive male.

"Please," I heard myself mumble, "don't tell anyone he did this."

The man flipped his cell phone open and continued on his way, tailed by his dog. When I got upstairs and saw the second bite, on the top of an abashed Libro's head, my better self took over.

"You know, Libro," I said, antiseptic in one hand, "you can't do that, bad dog, but actually, I don't like the man much myself."

JUST AFTER LABOR DAY Libro and I were in print. The full-page photograph was extraordinary, with Libro taking up the entire foreground, and myself, in baseball cap and high-tops, second fiddle behind him. He was bathed in magical light, as though a heavenly spotlight had found him. I called the photographer and apologized heartily.

I tried to explain the provocative and fleeting nature of fame to Libro.

"*Siéntate,*" I said.

He sat. We were out on the terrace and he had his wary eye on a circling fly.

"Look at me," I said. "This is important. Lie down."

I told him that when I was five, my mother showed me a small, shiny photograph of my uncle in the war standing beside his jeep. On the jeep was written, in huge letters: WEEZIE. That was my nickname. So, I deduced, since my uncle was far away in the Pacific and my name was so large on that jeep, I was famous all over the world. It took me a long time to understand differently. Why should Libro do better?

I've known what it's like to be on the street at ten in the morning, made-up and dressed up after an appearance on a television show, wondering what to do with myself, feeling forlorn. There is nothing left to do but to go home, wash the makeup off, and resume life. I wanted to warn Libro, prepare him for the seductive roller coaster to come.

Into his trusting amber eyes, I delivered the news: tomorrow, you'll be a star and then in less than a month, the magazine will be off the stands and we'll be ordinary civilians again. He just wagged his stumpy tail. So I gave him a biscuit and hoped his comedown wouldn't be too painful.

He didn't believe me, and for good reason.

To CELEBRATE OUR APPEARANCE in the magazine, we rode to midtown in a car (not a limo, as hoped) sent by the magazine's editor. We were given passes by the building guard. Some people in the lobby backed away as we went through. I heard a woman mutter, "pit bull!" With a visitor tag on his neck, Libro crowded everyone else aside to ride the elevator with his nose flat against the door. The magazine staff had spread bowls of doggy treats on the floor of the editor's office and some had brought their dogs in for the day. But Libro was the star, wandering in and out of offices, sniffing wastebaskets, encouraging petting. He was way too excited to eat.

"Visitor from another planet?" quipped a passerby, eyeing the tag that still flapped around his neck as we came out of the building onto Fifth Avenue. Libro ignored the comment, heading for the Armani boutique. The liveried doorman actually welcomed him in — in this city, smart people know that the guy in scruffy jeans might just turn out to be Bruce Springsteen or the woman with dirty hair and sunglasses Goldie Hawn. Few high-end shops or restaurants are actually as restrictive as you might think about who is welcome. Goldie could probably carry a pet iguana under her arm into Armani's.

I kept a close and wary eye on Libro, who I knew to be a compulsive shopper, an uptown *arriviste* pretending to be at ease in the world of swank. I made him sit while I examined a sweater. He sniffed every corner, and the salespeople paid him no mind. Luckily, he didn't have a penny on him and no credit cards, either. The doorman saluted as we left.

By the time we got to Central Park, Libro was dragging a stuffed scruffy yellow Big Bird he'd found outside Bergdorf's. We had become a Fellini film. He dragged Big Bird all the way across the park, dropping it on the sidewalk on Central Park West. I supposed another dog would inherit it. I hailed a cab and it stopped to pick us up. Fame has its perks.

When we alit on Broadway, the Indian man who runs the local stationery store saluted us. "Hey," he said, "Somebody put his picture in a magazine!" Nick from next door, halfway up the street, on his way to a job interview, was as excited as if I'd published a trenchant piece of cultural analysis in *Salon*. Phoenix's parents made me promise to give them an autographed copy of the magazine—meaning they wanted Libro's paw print on it.

But jealousy was also alive and well on the upper west side. Elvis the sheepdog turned his head away when Libro approached. Lola ran in the opposite direction. The mystery writer snorted and never read the piece. One of the local dog-walkers said she'd like to see the story, would I get her a copy? I said it was on the newsstands. She wanted a personal Xerox, don't ask why.

Among the people I hadn't heard from in years who came out of the woodwork were Annette and Eve, theatrical producers, who left a message on my answering machine about how shocked, absolutely shocked, they were to discover I was a "dog person."

"I'm not," I replied when I returned the call. "I am just

falling in love with *this* dog." It sounded, even to me, like the voice of someone who says, "I'm not a lesbian, I'm just in love with this one woman."

SINCE IT WASN'T QUITE a career to spend all my time playing with my dog, I'd accepted an invitation to lecture on women's history at a college in Utah. Libro would spend the week I was gone with my friend Antonia in New Jersey. I packed my own suitcase and then I packed his. At the sight of the green and white canvas bag, he raced back and forth around the room, making noises that were the canine equivalent of "whoopee!" When Antonia pulled up to our front door in her red Jeep, he leaped in. I handed Antonia the bag. Libro looked back at me, forlorn on the sidewalk, for only a second, then pressed his nose against the front window, eager to go.

In the cab to the airport, at the gate, then nestled into my seat, a current of giddy energy ran through me. I was free! Didn't have to walk the dog or buy him food or say no all day long. I could have adult, sophisticated conversations with people instead of asking about the best ear cleaning fluids or the efficacy of vitamin C powder. I could talk about books and mean books, not dogs. By the time I changed planes in Atlanta, passing by the pay phones with only a smidgin of desire to call Antonia and see if they made the trip okay, I was alert to any attractive men sitting nearby.

On the platform of a large lecture hall in Salt Lake City two days later, finishing up the part of my talk about the friendship of Elizabeth Cady Stanton and Lucretia Mott, mommy anxiety struck. I had described the reunion of Stanton and Mott in Seneca Falls, New York, in 1848 and was about to segue into an account of the first women's rights convention they organized together, but my mind was seized by images of Libro too upset to eat. The food bowl was full. He looked haggard. He whined.

I stumbled through the women's rights convention, hitting the right note as I described antislavery fighter Frederick Douglass rising to defend the women's demand for the vote, but I gave short shrift to the rest of the story. My attention was in New Jersey. I smiled through the reception, then raced back to my hotel room to telephone.

Libro was fine. Eating, sleeping, and everything else. Racing around in the woods. Antonia had taken him to the local mall that afternoon. In the store called Pet Nosh, waiting in line to pay for his pigs ears ("watch him," I'd warned, "he's a shoplifter"), a woman had recognized him.

"Oh my God," she'd shrieked, "I just saw that dog's picture in a magazine!"

So they were well, but I wasn't. Tossing in my hotel bed, flicking the TV on and off with the remote glued to my bedside table, my fingers buzzed with a memory of touching. The soft spot behind his ear, the gristle of his chin. I was sunk. I missed my dog.

Libro in Love

. . . .

On a cool Sunday morning, we saw the man with the dachshund, who'd skirted our photo shoot in the park. They were sitting on the bench in front of Café 104 on Broadway, the dog on the man's lap, nibbling at his neck. People on brunch dates were eating inside, and others were lining up for coffees, muffins, and bagels to take away. Dogs were tethered around the entrance — three cocker spaniels at a fire hydrant, a yapping white terrier near the bench, a mongrel asleep on his paws near the door. It looked like a hitching post outside a Western saloon.

Avoiding the terrier, I tied Libro's leash to the foot of the bench and asked the man, who was eating a chocolate-covered pastry, if he'd keep an eye on him. I always do that, no matter who is sitting there. When I came out of the café with my blueberry muffin, Libro and the dachshund were on the ground and the little ginger-colored frankfurter dog was energetically humping my celebrity boxer. Libro's expression was that tolerant and vaguely bored look. Oh, the things we beautiful people have to put up with.

The man was laughing. He wore jeans and a Hawaiian print shirt, three buttons undone, and sandals. He had nice toes and a day's worth of stubble on a dromedary face. He looked tired. I sat down. His dog kept humping mine.

The protocol is to talk about the dogs. We did. Mickey had grown up in the wilds of New Jersey, with dogs. His dachshund was male, ten years old, named Rex, scarred on his hindquarters where a pit had bitten him in Central Park early in the summer. We talked about who his vet was and what his diet was—Rex had to compete with two cats, especially at mealtimes. I thought *Rex* an ironically grandiose name for the small dog, until Mickey asked if I knew the Louis Armstrong story.

"Well, Armstrong is playing a gig in London and after he's finished the set, he comes out for the encore, sniffing that white handkerchief . . ."

"Which was full of cocaine," I said. Some things I know.

"Right. And he looks up at the box, where the royal family is sitting. You're not supposed to acknowledge the presence of royalty, so Armstrong looks up there and says, 'This one's for you, Rex.'"

I told Libro's far less witty but more touching tale, exaggerating my helplessness. My muffin was long gone and Mickey had gone inside to get a cup of coffee—he moved like a basketball player—which he sipped from a pink plastic cup while Libro licked his face. Rex was more reticent toward me, ducking his head when I picked him up. Mickey threw the cup away and picked up Libro's leash, putting one end in the dog's mouth and tugging from his end.

This was Libro's favorite game and he mostly tried to get men to play it with him. I thought he might want a daddy or it was simple testosterone bonding. Libro backed away, teeth clenched on the leash, crouched, growling. Mickey growled and pulled. Libro snapped his head from side to side. Mickey held fast. People stopped to watch and laugh. Libro yanked and got yanked in return. When, after ten minutes, the dachshund jumped off my lap and started barking, the game was over. Libro was more gracious than usual about it.

That's how Libro and I met Mickey and Rex. He was a musical arranger and jazz composer who'd moved to the neighborhood after a decade in a loft on the lower east side. He'd been away for most of the summer, working on a movie sound track in L.A. He didn't mention a wife or lover, of either sex. He allowed as how he'd seen Libro and me some weeks back, wandering in Riverside Park with a photographer and entourage. I told him about the magazine story and we all walked to the newsstand, where he bought a copy. My heart was his.

So was Libro's. He was glued to Mickey. As tall man and small dog turned right, east toward Central Park and their home, I struggled to drag Libro left. He sat down, defiantly, keeping his eyes on them until they were out of sight. I tried to be a little more diffident, a little more cool, but the truth is I felt the same way. I trusted Libro's instincts, perhaps more than my own.

He called. Although I would surely have called him, that very night, Mickey called and sang to me, sitting at his piano just three blocks away, a Sinatra medley. Set 'em up Joe. Libro sat at my feet, ears twitching and a very smug look on his face. The next day, Mickey faxed. He'd gone fishing in New Jersey and drawn a picture of the catch. What could I do but invite him to come cook it chez moi?

"They just don't make 'em like that anymore," I told Libro.

I cleaned up the house, fast. I bought salad and chilled a chablis. They arrived just as the sun was setting at eight, Mickey in a black T-shirt, jeans, sandals, a baseball cap, and a glowing tan, carrying several pounds of cleaned bluefish wrapped in newspaper. Rex gave me a perfunctory sniff and headed straight for Libro. I lit the briquettes in the grill on the terrace. The moonflowers opened.

I've pretty much learned not to interpret everything that happens to me, to resist the impulse to force life's random events into a narrative. I try to live one day at a time, appreciating what is, in the moment. "Now we're in this place," as Billy Crystal likes to say. But while I was profoundly appreciating Mickey, Rex, Libro, fish, and salad with chives and basil cut from patio pots, I was also telling myself a story.

Libro had fallen into my life for a reason and it was my task to understand it. I toyed with the idea that he was my familiar, as the witches call the animal companions who are both their servants and their masters. I'd been content in my life, but not inspired, not powerful. He had, perhaps, come to bring back the magic.

Surely, he'd opened my heart. Perhaps Libro was a

harbinger of great romance, real partnership. Maybe living with him was practice for the daily bliss of a new human companion, who might just be named Mickey.

I CLEARED THE TABLE while Rex humped Libro and Mickey asked where the filters were so he could make the coffee. Afterward, we walked the dogs along Riverside Drive. Libro raced and Rex waddled. We passed Josie, Elvis, and a young pit named Commodore, all ambling, leashed to their humans. We saw Dorothy, the walker, with two charges. Mickey knew none of the people or the dogs because he lived near Central Park, an entirely different canine society. To anyone watching, I was sure, we were just Louise and Libro strolling with another dog person and pup. Happened all the time. Didn't mean a thing.

Libro sped ahead, then burst into a huge, circular near-gallop, the way people suddenly burst into song. Pure puppy joy. But he came running back to check that Mickey and, almost an afterthought, I, were still there.

We stopped to talk to Jennifer, who was walking Blackie, her border collie. Libro lay down. He was used to this. Blackie lay down too. Rex cowered behind Mickey's leg. That night's installment in Jennifer's tale of perpetual woe was about her husband and the dog. Other nights, it had been about the daughter who refused to go to school, or Jennifer's mother withholding money, or an array of aches, pains, and diseases I could hardly keep count of. Often, though, the trouble was about her husband and the dog, separately and together. When her husband came home—which he only sometimes did, having a propensity for drunken benders and disappearing acts—Blackie peed on the floor, right at his feet. I sympathized with Blackie and suspected that Jennifer secretly did too. This night, however, Blackie had peed directly on the husband's shoe, and he, instead of assaulting the dog or telling Jennifer she had to take him to the pound, had stalked out.

Dorothy, the walker, passed by with two black poodles in tow while we were listening to the tale. Our eyes met. Dorothy's rolled with sympathy and she kept walking. Many dog people crossed the street when they saw Jennifer coming, but my little foursome was trapped.

Mickey was listening with a look of sympathy on his long face.

"Maybe you should check the local bars," he said.

"Fuck'm," Jennifer replied, "I don't care if that asshole never comes back. C'mon, Blackie."

She walked away.

THE NEXT DAY, I went to Mickey's place overlooking Central Park for breakfast. I went without Libro and felt slightly guilty about how easily I dismissed my pard-

ner for a man. It really was, I told myself, a question of lo-
gistics, a downtown appointment at midday, no time to
bring the dog home.

When I got there, Mickey was bare-chested, wearing
jeans and flip-flops, hair still wet from the shower. I
wanted to lick his face, his neck, his chest hair, his arms,
and lean against his long legs. Instead, I took a tour.

One bedroom full of recording equipment, the other
with nothing but a mattress on the floor. The piano, which
dominated the living room, was piled with scores, letters,
bills, videotapes, newspapers, and a medley of hats—
baseball caps, fedoras, a gondolier's straw. Under the piano
were three food bowls, Rex's pink ball tucked in one.
There was a Groucho Marx poster on the wall, two fishing
rods in a corner, and half-unpacked cartons scattered
around, black T-shirts spilling out of one. In deference to
my allergies, Mickey had locked the cats in the bathroom.
On the sound system, a combo played Coltrane with such
auditory nuance they might have been in the next room.
There were speakers everywhere, including, I assumed, the
bathroom, where the cats were probably jiving.

There were no signs of a woman. I looked. The clos-
ets seemed empty. No flowers anywhere. The bathroom,
a terrain worth investigating, was off limits because of
the cats.

He'd baked oat bran muffins. The tin still sat on a formica counter in the half-kitchen, burnt edges and all. And he'd brewed coffee in a French plunger pot. We sat on the living room floor. I moved a stack of old *Downbeat* magazines out of the way. Mickey handed me a muffin and then pushed the plunger in the coffeepot slowly, his dark eyes full of unmistakable meaning.

We made love on the floor, clothes scattered, with Rex trying to crawl into the middle of it. I was in such a deep swoon, I couldn't tell if the wet kisses on my face came from Mickey or his dog. At some point, Mickey gently lifted Rex, carried him to the bedroom, and shut the door. As we cooled off and came down in each other's arms, the place was smooth with the sounds of "Take the A Train," a whining dog behind one closed door, and two cats behind another.

Later, I had to face Libro. So much for Butch and Sundance, who never let a lover come between them. I climbed the stairs of my building with a mixture of happiness and guilt. Carefully, I opened the door. He jumped off the couch, tail wagging, and licked my leg. I bent down to scratch behind his ears. Could he smell the sex, still clinging to my body? If he could, it energized him, for he raced to his toy basket and came back holding the brown teddy bear in his mouth by one of its arms. He shook the bear ferociously, then flung it in the air and left it to run to the toy basket again, rummage around, and come back with a red plastic, squeaky lamb chop, which he held out to me.

"Drop it," I said.

He clenched his teeth around the lamb chop, jaw muscles rippling.

"Drop it."

He did, at my feet, and I flung it across the room. He got it and proudly brought it back.

"Drop it."

We were going to be okay.

Family Values

....

Libro, Rex, Mickey, and I became a foursome, easy as that. It had taken Peter two years and a lot of work on my part before he came closer. We broke up after our first weekend together. Then we had a coast-to-coast commuting relationship. He eventually moved from San Francisco to New York, saying it was because the professional opportunities were better. He sublet an apartment clear on the east side and way downtown, an hour away. We broke up. We got together. He started leaving things at my place, then he lost his sublet. Never quite saying he wanted to move in, Peter seeped in, hanger by hanger, until he had his own keys and the greeting on my answering machine said "we" could not come to the phone. Every time I turned my key in the lock, I thought he might have moved out.

With the dogs, Mickey and I took walks and ate meals. Without them, we went to movies and made out on streetcorners and subway platforms. Lovemaking was in his place or mine, mostly in the daytime, because of the need to feed the cats and walk the dog, he said. It made no sense. He liked to tinker at his piano late at night. I would have taken Libro out for an evening trot and left him home alone while I slept at Mickey's until the sun was up, but it didn't happen. Piano tinkering.

MICKEY HAD A SMALL, ratty car, green, with rust stains, which delighted Libro to no end. All cars delighted him. Anyone who parked on our street risked opening a door to find a brindled creature sitting politely, tail wagging, and an unmistakable appeal for a ride on his face. The start of summer weekends had been treacherous times to be in the streets with him, with people loading children, baggage, bicycles, canoes, and in-laws into their vehicles, carelessly leaving car doors open as they did so, unaware that Libro had spotted an opportunity half a block away. Well behaved though he was, he could pull the leash out of my hands if he really wanted to, and an open car door made him really want to, head lowered, neck straining, shoulders tensed, as though the love of his life or his last meal were waiting down the street.

Although most people thus assaulted laughed and shooed him out of their cars, this naked desire for transport embarrassed me, as though it reflected badly on his homelife or on my ability to provide, and so I lied.

"No, Libro," I'd say. "This is not your car. Out."

Passion clouded Libro's judgment. There was a man who lived in one of the big prewar apartment houses on West End Avenue, a lawyer who had been disbarred for sexually harassing a woman who worked in his firm and a female client. The way I'd heard it, he'd raped the client, but bargained away a criminal charge in exchange for leaving the law. He haunted the streets, a tall, good-looking white man in his forties, always chewing gum, wearing a black down parka even on warm days. He supposedly had a wife and children, but I never saw them. I did see the old black Chevy van, which he moved from one side of the street to the other on alternate days.

Libro saw the van too, from the inside. I'd been struggling along the street with a fifteen-pound bag of laundry in one arm, trying to hold onto Libro's leash with my other hand as he investigated the aromas at the base of various buildings. He'd apparently missed the training lessons on how to heel. Suddenly the van drew alongside us and the man asked if he could help. Although my mother told me never to get into cars with strangers and although I knew the man's reputation, I had a ferocious dog with me, my arms were throbbing, and so I said yes.

Inside, there were stacks of newspapers and a mattress. Libro sniffed everything and then curled up and put his head down on the sheets. Leon, as the lawyer turned out to be called, sometimes slept in his van, parking it on a turnout off the West Side highway, because he needed to get away from his family. He was writing a memoir about how he had been "Clintonized," meaning, in his terms, falsely accused of sexual misconduct by lying women, and would I like to read it? All this on the five-block drive to the laundry. I left Libro inside, with Leon scratching the dog's head, while I delivered the bundle to the Korean woman inside, and then I had to drag the dog out of the van to walk home. I told Leon I was too busy just then to read the memoir.

But Libro was never too busy for Leon and his van. If I saw him coming and tried to cross the street, Libro would dig his heels in and sit down. Every time we passed the parked black hulk, Libro got up on his hind legs and scratched at the door.

So when, in early October, Libro learned that Mickey had a car, I knew we were done for. He climbed obediently into the back seat. Rex sat on Mickey's lap. We drove to Coney Island, where I had long ago gritted my teeth and proven my courage by riding the Parachute Jump and the Cyclone with my father.

The amusement park I remembered now lay in ruins, shuttered, fading, decrepit, and surprisingly small. Mickey had proven his courage in very different ways—by being the weird kid in school, writing songs and poems when his friends were out playing baseball. The collapsed amusements meant nothing to him. The ocean did.

Like me, he loved the briny smell and the splashing surf. The ocean had not decayed, nor the wide sand beach, where some intrepid souls lay bundled up on beach blankets and two figures in wet suits dove into the crashing waves. We walked with our arms around each other and our shoes off, Rex darting in and out of the water's edge, Libro keeping on dry land. The dogs fell asleep on the drive back to Manhattan, Rex on Mickey's lap while he drove, Libro in the backseat, snoring. It was hard not to think of us as a potential family, one cockamamie enough for me to live with.

MICKEY HAD A WAY with dogs, clowning around not only with his and mine, but somehow hypnotizing the passing canines so their owners had to yank their leashes to get them to face forward and keep moving. Although I had fallen in love with Libro and felt incredibly close to him, I knew I was a person and he was a dog. As surely as Butch and Sundance are bonded but separate, I knew the difference between Libro and me. Not Mickey. He could become a dog. He spoke their language, with whines, growls, and silent stares. He squeaked at Rex, on Rex's pitch, and the little dog answered. He boxed Libro in the side like a four-footed boxer himself, and when Mickey panted, with his tongue hanging down, it was almost frightening to me, although gullible Libro could hardly keep himself on the ground.

I wouldn't have noticed a man who was without a canine, leery as past experience had left me on the subject of romantic triangles. Me, he, and Libro did not compute. Louise, Mickey, Libro, and Rex did. The glitches seemed small enough: Mickey's apartment was cluttered and chaotic, he was a little tight-fisted about money, and we still had not spent a night together. When we got back from Coney Island, I, full of family feeling, proposed to do so, but Mickey wanted to work on a new song. My tolerance was waning.

Libro knew something was wrong when we got up the four flights of stairs and I sank into the couch and turned on the television set. He sat beside me and fell asleep curled in my lap. Mickey called at midnight. The song was about walking near the sea with me.

If I'd known the words to the "Hallelujah Chorus," I'd have been singing them. I'd probably have tried to teach Libro too. Judging from the way he leaped up at the sound of the doorbell, the phone, or the fax in the weeks that followed, however, I think he already knew them.

LIFE WAS BIG NOW, crammed with dogs, neighbors, my friends, Libro's friends, my work, Mickey's work, sex, and love. I couldn't remember what it had been like before—what did I do with all that time alone?—and I kept waiting for it to feel like too much for me.

As a modern woman with some experience, I know about boundaries. You have to decide what to let in, how much you can give. A full heart is wonderful; a bursting heart leads to intensive care. I had pretty much taught Libro to leave me alone when I was working, but I knew that if he got sick or hurt, he'd be my priority, whatever was going on. So would Mickey, whose own boundaries seemed as solid as the walls of Masada.

Dating with dogs was new turf. Even Miss Manners ignored it in her etiquette book. I was not Libro's mommy, and I was determined not to become Rex's stepmommy. I wouldn't discipline Rex or make suggestions about his diet and I really didn't want to be saddled with dog-sitting when Mickey went away. Was I cruel?

Once when Mickey was sorting through some papers, he showed me a get-well card a former girlfriend had sent Rex on the occasion of his surgery.

"Did she have a dog of her own?" I asked.

She hadn't. She also hadn't had much of a life of her own, I surmised, when Mickey described how she'd moved from Florida to live with him, hoping to get a band together and be the lead singer, but ending up booking his gigs, doing his errands, and ingesting a lot of cocaine. A boundary problem. After rehab some years back, she'd left.

MY FEARS WERE UNFOUNDED. When Mickey went to L.A. on a four-day business trip, Rex went to a friend's place in Westchester. He called me every night and faxed during the day. I faxed back.

Mornings, Libro and I romped in Riverside Park, where the trees flashed russet, crimson, and vermilion, and the dogs, invigorated by the cooler weather, zipped around as though amphetamines had been dispensed at the park stairs. Tony, who had a dog named Pookie, was a sweet, overweight union organizer; he suddenly appeared attached to an oxygen tank, which he wheeled along one side while he held his mutt on a leash with the other. I heard from the dog people that he had emphysema, but

Tony never mentioned it, just rolled the tank, held onto Pookie, and talked about city politics.

I'd seen Libro licking his bad leg and called the ASPCA vet. She assured me that licking—Libro had looked "caught"—didn't necessarily mean pain. He might have been cleaning himself, catlike. I had learned from a boy on my street how to squeeze the sides of Libro's mouth so I could get it open and slide an aspirin back into his throat and I was sure he was improving. I started thinking about acupuncture.

But here he was, racing up and down the hills, in mad pursuit of squirrels trying to set themselves up for the coming winter. You'd never know. His body was thicker, especially in the chest, where the paintbrush-shaped splash of white was expanding. He was buff, a hunk. A woman with an overweight collie asked to borrow Libro as a trainer for her lazy mutt.

We usually went out in the middle of the day, along the Drive, past children in the playground wearing sweaters, or on Broadway, where the cafés were packing up their sidewalk tables. We did our errands. Weekday daytime belonged to people like me, as well as to the re-tired, the unemployed, the nannies, and the dog-walkers. Lola had a professional walker, but all the other dogs trotted around, usually in packs of three or four, with neighborhood dog-owning women earning a little something on the side.

I'd once heard a lunatic babbler in line at the post office, pointing at a woman with a baby carriage and saying in a perfectly conversational tone: "See that woman. You know what her husband has to make for her to stay home with the child all day? You know what kind of income it takes to support a whole family? See that woman . . ." He might have been a London School of Economics escapee, and he was absolutely right. The people who lived with the dalmation named Byron had a newborn and so did the mutt Luther's people, but I never saw any of them around during the day. The grown-ups worked. The babies had nannies. Byron and Luther, I presumed, had discipline.

The shopkeepers had time, and the wise ones, knowing their markets, had dog biscuits. The manager at Love Cosmetics fed Libro treats and so did the dry cleaner and the local thrift shop, but the Korean grocer, who said that in his country, striped canines like mine were called Tiger Dogs, worried about his cat and waited impatiently for Libro to leave. The pizza guys gave me barely warm slices to get me out fast. The woman at the laundry cowered. Libro, who apparently remembered only good things and let go of the bad, believed that all stores doled out biscuits, which caused him to sit looking bewildered while the locksmith copied my keys and did no more than say, "nice doggy."

In cartoons, the dog barks at the postman, but not in my life. In my life, the dog wagged his tail, tried to pee on the mail cart, and sat quietly while Jerry, the mail carrier, and I talked about the Knicks, Saddam Hussein, the screeching opera singer in the building next door, and apartment rental prices. Jerry, who lived in the Bronx, where he cared for a brother dying of AIDS, spoke Spanish to Libro and English to me. Without Libro dragging me into the streets, the shopkeepers would have been generic and the postman, the Fed Ex guy, and the man in the UPS truck merely the people who bring the mail.

Libro glared at me when I turned back toward our building and sometimes he sat down belligerently on the sidewalk. Brief and busy afternoon outings weren't enough for him, but they were for me. I was still figuring out whose life it was, his or mine, on a case-by-case basis.

Evenings, when he got back from L.A., I walked over to Mickey's and we took both dogs to Central Park, where other people with dogs, most still wearing their daytime suits or dresses, hosiery, and jackets, nodded or saluted, but never stopped to talk. They were mostly busy on their cell phones. It was dark by seven, abruptly, with little protracted twilight.

THE HOMELESS PEOPLE WERE setting up cardboard tents in their enclave near 108th Street. Some of the same people came back night after night, including Cedric, whom I didn't recognize at first because he had cut his dreadlocks. But Libro knew him. Newcomers to the tent city flinched at the sight of a drooling dog bounding toward them.

"Git him away," one man yelled. "I'm ascared of dogs."

Cedric to the rescue.

"Yo, homes. How ya been?" he croaked, as Libro lapped his face.

To me he said, "How's his leg?"

"Better."

"Ya know, homes, it's gettin' cold. You gotta have a sweater or somethin'. I'm gonna get you a sweater."

Sweaters were the future, but Libro only cared about the present. He sniffed the big green trash bags in which Cedric's crew carried their stuff. He tried to get a sip of beer from a man lounging on a bench, propped on one elbow, sleeping bag over his legs, but I intervened.

"No, Libro! Off! Come here!"

The exclamation points worked. He came. As we wandered away, the man on the bench said, "nice dog," and the man who was afraid said, "yeah, he'd make a nice roast."

A Chill in the Air

•••••••••••••

For Halloween, the dog community went into parox-
ysms of creativity. In the afternoon, there was a costume
competition at the dog run, won by two fat white bulldogs dressed as a Lord and Lady. The Lord wore a shiny
black top hat and starched tuxedo bib, the Lady a frilly
pink tutu and veil. Libro refused to participate. I'd
thought of dressing him as a biker with a glittering stud
in his ear or even of putting satin boxer trunks on him,
but he would have none of it. He kicked his hind legs
and tore at the trunks with his front paws until I released him, and I never got to invent his biker costume.

That evening, Mickey wore a dark suit, white shirt,

black tie, gray fedora, and a Freddie Kruger mask, which scared the hell out of Libro. We drove downtown to the Greenwich Village Halloween parade. Rex had on a Yankees T-shirt, so large it dragged on the ground and a backwards cap, held to his head by an elastic band. I'd done myself up as a biker chick: long blond wig, heavy makeup, including a beauty mark and bright red lipstick, tough black leather jacket, miniskirt, cheap perfume. Libro went as a nudist.

We paraded up Sixth Avenue with an array of drag queens, stilt-walkers, and several Monica Lewinskys. A Latin band played "La Macarena" behind us, and, behind them, a platoon of people with AIDS rode in wheelchairs. Mickey worked the railings, muttering "I know where you live" at the front row of spectators. Rex wriggled in and out of people's legs, and Libro wagged his tail nonstop, pulled at his leash, and tried to sniff everyone in the crowd. By Fourteenth Street, Mickey was carrying Rex, saving him from being crushed by the stiletto heels of the passing drag queens.

We left long before the parade's end, missing the bacchanal on Christopher Street, which would have been too much for the dogs. I sat in the backseat of the car, holding an exhausted Libro on my lap, feeling sour. I loved the dense late-night lunacy of the Christopher

Street party, the street closed off, the drag queens party-
ing with abandon, flaunting an outrageous campiness
now missing from the toned-down official parade. Dogs
could be a drag. So could men who wouldn't spend the
night, a habit of Mickey's I was growing tired of.

Mickey was revved, singing and chattering all the way
uptown, still wearing his mask. He parked on my street
and, with no discussion or persuasion, carried Rex upstairs, walking behind me with his free hand on my ass,
murmuring, "I know where you live." Worn-out Libro still
managed to demonstrate his delight at Mickey's presence.

We put the dogs together in my study, Libro on his
fluffy bed, Rex on a thick towel under my desk. We set a
second bowl of fresh water beside Libro's. I closed the
door firmly. In the bedroom, Mickey and I swam in the
sea of bliss and fell asleep in each other's arms. I awoke
snuggled on his chest, my toes against his calves, his
scent permeating the sheets. Mickey, eyes open, stared at
the ceiling in what looked like panic.

"What's wrong?" I said. I never learn.

He followed the age-old script—saying "nothing,"
turning his eyes away, but eventually, after I'd gotten up
and made coffee and brought him a cup, he squeezed out,
"I just don't know how to fit this into my life."

"Ah," I said. I understood.

I kissed his eyelids and would have done and asked more, but Rex was madly yelping in my office, so I got up and went to get the dogs. Libro lay on his bed pashalike, with Rex trying to climb on his back. He had that bored/ adored look on his face. One water bowl was empty, the other untouched.

Rex scrambled past my legs and went to find Mickey; Libro sniffed me and boxed my leg. I bent down to scratch him behind his ears and he buried his head in my crotch, tail wagging. Then he too went to find Mickey, who was pouring another cup of coffee in the kitchen.

We went out alone, an urgent Libro and I, our feet crunching in the dried leaves on the ground. The air felt cold. In the dog run, a woman with a little white poodle reported that Lola had won a ribbon at a show in Pennsylvania. Josie arrived, with a new haircut, her coat flat, curly, and shiny, like a Persian lamb. She looked sleek and ladylike. When Libro tried to roughhouse with her, she demurred. I liked her tomboy spirit better.

We returned to an apartment empty of man and dog. Libro raced from living room to bedroom, poking under the bed, sniffing the sheets, galloping into my office. Mickey's note on the kitchen counter said, "Call you later."

• • •

BEFORE I KNEW IT, that terror known as "the holidays" had sneaked up on us. Wooden slats were being hammered into place to hold the forests of Christmas trees soon to clutter every piece of sidewalk outside every grocery store in the neighborhood. At 110th Street and Broadway, some enterprising Canadians were occupying half a block with blue spruces and Douglas firs. Cyclamen and the occasional poinsettia appeared in the florist's window. There was stew on the menu at the corner café.

Some dogs appeared in the park in winter clothes— acrylic sweaters or tartans—except for Lola, who had a purple felt coat that made her look like a racehorse.

I'd had my own wardrobe crisis, wearing light gray sweatpants to a muddied Riverside Park, wising up and acquiring blacks and greens from the local thrift shop. From the floor of my closet I reclaimed a ratty black parka, bits of feathered stuffing poking through holes invisible to the naked eye.

"How do you know when a dog needs a sweater?" I asked the dog people.

"Is he shivering?"

"Does he want to go back inside?"

He wasn't. He didn't. Libro loved the cold. When we got indoors and I rubbed his chest, it was warm. The tips of his ears felt chilly and so did mine.

From mid-November through the day after New Year's, my neighbors and the dog people in the park were planning or going to parties, taking trips, or doing things *en famille*, which sometimes meant with parents and other times meant with children. Some of my friends were worrying about not planning or going to parties, not caring or pretending not to care. The twelve-steppers stepped up their meetings. The boys next door had a huge turnover of visitors, usually ruddy-complexioned young men lugging heavy backpacks and bedrolls who rang the wrong doorbell in our building, which is how I got to meet them. There were a lot of pizza deliveries.

When I was single and not romantically involved, I'd mobbed myself up so entirely, stuffing the "important" days with family difficulties, dear friends, and boring acquaintances, suffering a January hangover akin to having binged on empty calories for weeks. Peter and I had "done" the holidays with flickering menorah, festive tree, and groaning sideboards for several years, and once, to escape, flown to Kuala Lumpur, where New Year's was celebrated by a pots and pans parade in the streets. I'd felt spiritual and peaceful, withdrawn and depressed, and now I wasn't sure what I was.

Libro made a difference. Energized by the chill in the air and all the bustle in the streets and in our building, he raced everywhere, tugging me so hard I considered buy-ing a choke chain. I prayed for a snowy winter, just for the pleasure of the chiaroscuro, his dark coat a blur across a frosted landscape. I couldn't trek over the river and through the woods to grandma's house unless Libro could trek too. Besides, grandma was dead.

Mickey made a difference too. Unlike regular people, entertainers are busier at holiday times, so I'd not seen him much during the day, but he and Rex spent the night once or twice a week. He brought a towel for Rex to sleep under. People from L.A. were coming to town, gigs were on tap. He was trying to fit it all into his life. All of a sud-den, I didn't seem to be having quite so hard a time. How would little Rex look scurrying across the tundra?

Happy Holidays

· · · · · · · · · · · · · ·

My friend Diana and I decided to have our annual holiday brunch early, the week before Thanksgiving, because she and her husband were going to Alaska. Diana often goes alone on spiritual journeys to rain forests and deserts, but at holiday time, she buddies up with her husband of thirty years. We met at Café des Artistes, near Lincoln Center, halfway between our domiciles. She wore sheepskin, I wore down. The sky was gray, the restaurant windows steamed by the bonhomie within.

We had a small table in the crowded bar, near the front door, in front of the steamy windows. We ordered hot mulled wine and tried to talk over the din, but I was missing every third word and so I got up to go to the ladies' room and check out the more accommodating booths in the back room, where the Christie murals of naked ladies are. I walked up eight stairs and passed two booths before I saw Mickey.

He was facing me, leaning across the table toward a woman whose face I couldn't see. He had both hands on her face and his mouth pressed against hers. I felt his fingertips, his tongue. Our eyes caught. His said, oh shit, and he sat back. The woman turned, puzzled, a wide face framed by black curls, not very young. Then she turned back to him.

I kept walking toward them, dragging like a diver in a wet suit on the bottom of the ocean. Turning back didn't cross my mind. It took about five hours to reach their table. He had a grin on his face and looked positively goofy. She was wide-eyed and still puzzled. I found her no great beauty, which made it all the worse.

Mickey introduced us. "Clara," he said.

My mind worked slowly, but I'm cursed with near perfect recall. The way he'd told it, he'd been running late and forgotten his wallet. Clara had been passing by on a west-side street when Mickey had gotten out of a taxi only to discover he couldn't pay the fare. That was some years ago. She taught French at a private girl's school on the east side. He sometimes had dinner with her or went to a concert when she had tickets, which she got from her parents, who subscribed to everything in the city.

Everybody seemed to speak very slowly and from very far away. I opened my mouth to say something, but instead of words, I gagged, and out came that morning's breakfast, missing the snowy white edge of the tablecloth and pooling at my feet. I turned and ran.

"Let's get out of here," I told a startled Diana, "Mickey's in there with another woman."

She must have paid the check.

"I threw up on them," I said, the minute we were out the door.

"Well, nobody can accuse you of not being in touch with your feelings."

We walked to Lincoln Center and sat in the cold on the edge of the closed-down fountain. Reasonable Diana tried to suggest that the woman might be Mickey's cousin or an old friend, but she knows I'm not paranoid and that when your bones—or, in my case, your intestines— speak loudly, they usually tell the truth. I saw what I saw. I knew what I knew. We went to Forlini's, across Broadway, waited ten minutes for a table in the company of tourists speaking German and Russian, then walked out. We wandered a block away and around the corner to The Ginger Man, huddled in the humid, smoky bar, and left.

I went home.

There was a dog in my house. I ignored him.

I sat on the couch, besieged by flashbacks:

Mickey telling me he'd always had a woman, never been alone. Two wives; the Florida woman; a downstairs neighbor; Clara, who was supposed to be a long time ago and over, except for an occasional "friendly" cappuccino.

Me describing my distinctly nonvirginal wild and crazy youth and more narrow adulthood. Saying that I'd been alone since Peter left.

"Well," Mickey says, leaning over, "you were waiting for something real."

I remembered a Chinatown basement restaurant that we left before the meal arrived, rushing uptown to make love. Many meals. Dog-walks. His park and mine. The Metropolitan Museum, a room empty of people, filled with Dutch landscapes, where he put his hand under my dress, like a bad boy in the twelfth grade.

Libro sat at my feet, looking bewildered. I told him to go away. He climbed on the couch and licked my face. I sent him away. He came back. I took him by his collar and walked him to my study, where he sniffed a pink ball I'd bought for Rex and looked bewildered again. I picked the ball up, closed the door, and put the tinkly pink thing, whose sound had always annoyed me, in the garbage. Libro whined.

I walked around. There were four messages on my answering machine, none from Mickey, sonofabitch. Through the door, I told Libro to shut up. I was afraid I'd hit him. I got into bed and closed my eyes. It was 6:30 P.M. I forgot to feed the dog.

In the morning, very early, Libro was lying just behind the door, head on his front paws. There had been no accidents. His tail wagged. Right, I thought, we don't need Greek tragedy. I rubbed him, hugged him, fed him, and dressed in layers. He watched, jumping around, and rushed whooping down the stairs when I opened the apartment door, which I had forgotten to double lock.

Relief.

No one was up yet, but Starbucks was open on Broadway. No dogs were allowed, which meant we never went there, but this time, I tied Libro's leash around a parking meter and, watching him through the front window as he lay down with his chin on the sidewalk, ordered a latte to go. He jumped up when I returned and knocked the cup out of my hand. Life sucked. I went back inside, where the lone clerk in green apron had witnessed the accident and was whipping up another cup. Maybe life didn't suck so much.

We went to the park, where Libro raced ahead and I wished I had my running gear on. You can, I've learned, outrun pain. Overnight, though, the pain had muted and I was feeling what I thought of as reasonable. Maybe Diana was right, I'd overreacted, it was nothing or not much or irrelevant and did my life at this stage really depend on monogamy after all? I felt so calm by the time we got home, close to seven o'clock, that I fed Libro and sat down apologetically to talk with him while he chomped, before I checked my machine.

One message.

Ah.

It was Diana, at the airport.

So I called Mickey while Libro licked my leg. I spoke to a sleep-shrouded voice that agreed we should talk and would call back later. I went out again, alone, to outrun the pain. I came back with tears frozen on my face and rushed to the shower so Libro wouldn't see. He scratched at the bathroom door.

The showdown was just us, Mickey and me, at the corner café. No dogs. He kept his jacket on. He'd lied, big time. He'd been seeing Clara all along, for three years, and had moved uptown to be closer to her. He couldn't move in with her because her building wouldn't let Rex in and she wouldn't move in with him because she didn't want to lose her rent-controlled apartment. In another circumstance, I would have found these very New York

arrangements comic or even nonsensical. As he confessed
—he'd often been at her place before he went home and
called me at midnight—he kept looking at the door, like
Libro does when he wants to go out.

I kept my head down, listening to an unheard hum,
and read the menu fourteen times, wondering if Libro
would collapse if we spent the rest of the day walking
around outside in the cold. I longed for an Uzi, or the
strength to strangle, and wondered how I would tell
Libro, who had, after all, been betrayed too. I did listen
to Mickey's response to the dumbest question you can ask
in a situation like this: why? He couldn't help himself, he
said, he'd just been swept away.

So I swept myself away, out of the café, past a stand
of Christmas trees and down the windy street, having
plunked down my share of the bill, wishing I hadn't. I
trudged up the stairs, past the smell of a roast cooking in
Sophia's apartment and marijuana drifting beneath the
door to the boys' next door. Libro lay on his bed with
his eyes closed. I covered him with my body before he
had a chance to jump up and hugged him so tightly he
yelped.

"It's just you and me now, kid," I said.

He squirmed out from under me and banged on my
arm with his front paw.

"What do you want?"

I followed him to the kitchen. He stood over the empty plastic food and water bowls on the floor, looking down at them, up at me. Heartache was one thing, but dinner was another.

Cold

Winter White

. . . .

It was a week of wintry weather and white dogs. Friday morning, we met Pearl, a tiny female bulldog in heat, just adopted by a young blond woman. Pearl was deaf. She had a flat-nosed face, like Libro's, and she liked him right away, there on the corner of Riverside Drive, in a whipping wind. The young woman shivered in her wool shirt and sipped from an oversized coffee cup. I smelled snow in the air. Like many people walking with small dogs, the woman had flinched at Libro's large brown hunkered-down tiger-walking approach, pulling back on Pearl's leash, about to scoop her up, but the tails were wagging and Pearl tugged forward, so they met on the ground.

He sniffed her private parts, she reciprocated, and then he sniffed again. Neutered he was, but not without interest. She encouraged him, shamelessly. When he looked away, she pushed closer and won his heart, or perhaps just his nose. The woman wanted to get to work and out of the cold; Pearl wanted Libro's ardor. We walked up the street together, to West End Avenue, where they lived, the dogs almost glued, his nose to her rear. Pearl went inside the big apartment building. Libro sat down to wait. He was getting harder to pull along.

"*Levántate*," I said. Get up.

He sat, staring into the marble lobby.

"*Levántate*, Libro."

People walking their kids to the school bus, waiting for taxis, or hurrying to the subway in office clothes thought it was funny, me pulling at the dog, him stubbornly refusing to move, staring into the building as though he could will Pearl to reappear. "His new girlfriend lives here," I explained, as though the force of his passion explained and justified how powerless I was to control my own pup.

Saturday morning, as we crossed West End Avenue on our way to get a bagel and a newspaper on Broadway, a big fluffy white dog came toward us, alone, dodging the light traffic. I held my breath and grasped Libro's leash. We both watched the dog make its way to the curb, lift its leg against the building, and look around. Unneutered. I now knew how you can tell.

A young man went by on a bike, but it wasn't his dog, he said. We followed the white dog along the sidewalk, empty of pedestrians. He kept looking back at us.

"Sit," I yelled.

The dog sat where he was. So did Libro.

"Not you," I said. "Come."

We approached gingerly. The dog lay down and turned his head away. He had a green nylon collar, no tags. His long tail flapped back and forth on the sidewalk and he looked scared and hungry, but not wounded or sick. What did I know? Holding his collar, I walked him toward our building. He came along. Libro did too, placidly, but looking confused—we'd only just set out for our morning walk.

Life takes strange turns, I told him. There was not a soul on the street.

I found another dog, I said to the universe, now what do I do?

I might have done nothing, but I had already done something. Before I found Libro, I might not even have noticed, but now that I noticed, I would have been haunted if I'd walked on by. I was ruined.

I put the white dog in the small downstairs hallway,

under the mailboxes, and climbed the four flights with Libro, leaving him looking puzzled in our apartment while I went back down with a bowl of water for the white dog. He guzzled eagerly. I sat on the floor trying to talk to him, but he refused to make contact. Worried about leaving him in the hallway while I got help, but unwilling to commit to bringing him upstairs, I imagined a startled neighbor finding the dog and shooing him into the mean streets again. If only I had a Post-It: Please leave this dog here while I figure out what to do.

If you're a lost, stolen, abandoned, or runaway dog in Manhattan, don't get found on a weekend. Nobody will come to pick you up until Monday. I learned this after much frantic phoning. The dog rescuers must all have gone skiing in Vermont or Gstaad. Ah well, I thought, what's two days? Might be fun.

Libro was at the door, not the rascal Libro I knew and loved, the sweet little guy the neighborhood had adopted, but a ferocious tough, feet squared, chest thrust forward, ears tense, eyes glaring, growling and barking, full of rage and menace, blocking the threshold.

This was what I had in mind the first days after he came to live with me, one reason I decided to keep him —that he'd protect me in the house. Until now, however, he'd let me down on that score. He'd actually been a lover and a bit of a wuss. Not a single stranger who came to the door—FedEx pickup men, phone repair, Jehovah's Witnesses, UPS, the landlord's lawyer with a summons for rent due—had been met with anything but an invitation from Libro. Even two cops who had dropped, guns drawn, onto the terrace from the rooftop above, in pursuit of a rumored burglar scuttling along the rooftops.

"Hold the dog," they'd growled. "Hold the dog."

I'd held him, restraining his affection for police, who had saved his life, an affection he demonstrated whenever he saw uniforms on the street or when there was a patrol car stopped on the edge of Riverside Drive, its inhabitants stalking speeders and car thieves or just sipping coffee, reading the newspaper, and having a snack. With the gun-pointing cops crouched on my terrace, I controlled Libro's truly terrifying impulse to plant a wet kiss on each of their faces.

They never caught the burglar and I'd given up on Libro as a watchdog. Now, however, trying to edge the white dog into the apartment, I commanded this killer as sharply as I could to stop, sit, get down, chill out, and take a hike. Eventually, I got them squared away in separate rooms, but Libro was unappeasable and the white dog was mad as hell and not going to take it anymore. I didn't blame him, after all he'd been through.

I was afraid the noise would provoke someone to call the police.

The white dog was truly beautiful, with long soft hair already leaving traces on my floor, and piercing coal black eyes. I liked the look of the two dogs together, Libro's dark striping and the other's alabaster. I had a breathtaking picture in my mind of them romping in a snowy landscape. As fashion accessories, they were unbeatable.

Libro should have a roommate, I thought, another dog to take up the slack of my severe limitations. Then it wouldn't matter so much if I sometimes went away for hours at a time, tired of flinging plastic lamb chops and tugging on rope toys or that I made him sleep alone. He'd get used to the white dog; they'd be happy together.

Truth is, the absence of Mickey and Rex left a hole in our lives. Libro had spent the first week looking for them, sniffing around my studio, flattening himself to peer under the couch, extending his paw to feel what he could not see. He dashed into my bedroom, looked under the radiator, sniffed behind the dresser, and tried to press his nose on the pillowcases, until I told him to get down and off. Each time, not finding what he was hunting for, he furrowed his brow and looked to me for an explanation.

"They're gone," I said. "No more. *Nada más*. The guy was a bad guy. *Hombre muy malo*. Fageddaboudit."

Libro didn't get it.

In the street, he stopped at every dachshund, hairy and hairless, big and small. When I let him get close, he was disappointed, although he did make the acquaintance of a timid petite auburn dachshund named Zooey, after the J. D. Salinger character, whose owner carried him almost everywhere. On a rare occasion when Zooey was on the ground, Libro played gently while I reassured the terrified red-haired woman that my boxer had no intention of devouring her five-month-old sweetie. I thought at first the dog's name was Zoe, after the actresses Atkins or Caldwell, but it was a boy, Zooey, bright-eyed and frolicsome, but not interested in Libro the way Rex had been. Libro took what he could get.

Tall, lanky white men were also the object of Libro's expectant scrutiny, but his nose told him immediately they were not Mickey and he approached the men less frequently than he did the dogs.

I, on the other hand, wanted to be rid of Mickey and Rex. I'd whirled through the apartment that first night, eliminating all traces of man and dog. In the past, I might have clung to mirages of the "he'll change, he'll see" variety, but not this time. I'd waited far too long for my life with Peter to become happy-ever-after, and I wouldn't do it again. Out, damned spot, is closer to what I felt.

Out with the ratty towel Rex used as a blanket. Down came the photographs on the bulletin board of we happy four in various change-partner combinations: he with his, me with mine, he with mine, and so on. I tore them up before I threw them all away. Into the trash went the faxes, love notes, and poems. Libro thought the cleaning frenzy meant guests were coming and trotted to the door to wait.

Being angry probably saved me from crawling into bed for days on end, sinking into daytime TV, retelling the story to every sympathetic ear on the telephone, or finding a shrink. And Libro saved me too. I couldn't have cried around him even if I'd wanted to, because Libro's response to tears was smothering affection and an almost hysterical concern. Crying babies in their carriages in the street had been confronted with a set of paws and a tongue, hell-bent on helping, which only made them cry harder. He'd heard a baby's wail coming from a window in the apartment building on our corner one morning and sat, staring up at the window and refusing to move. My rare tears had elicited such overwhelming behavior that I'd stifled them just to appease Libro, in advance.

LIBRO'S COMPASSION, HOWEVER, was not stronger than his self-interest. With the white dog whimpering in the living room and Libro howling in my office, I spent a turbulent afternoon trying to comfort each of them. The white dog responded, lying on his front paws and napping, but Libro growled at the competitor's scent on my hands and bared his teeth. I hadn't seen him so frantic since the day I brought him home. This wasn't going to work, not even until Monday morning.

Over the din, I got on the phone, calling all the dog people whose numbers I had, trying to find someone to shelter Libro's nemesis for twenty-four hours. No luck. I took the white dog out, down to the park, past the dog run, but no one knew him or would take him. I did, however, get some good suggestions about what to do.

A few blocks away was an animal hospital. The receptionist had said on the phone that they didn't take strays, but I'd been told in the park that a dog left in the lobby there would not be put outside. White dog in tow, I lurked like a thief in front of the building. When the entryway was clear, I shoved the dog inside and ran off, afraid to look back. At home, Libro was peacefully asleep, snoring loudly. You're safe, I said. And I'll never do it again.

A SLOBBERING LOVER BOY as a matter of course, Libro now stayed closer to me than usual in the streets and went into deep but not obtrusive compassion mode at home. He cuddled on my lap, offering brief kisses, just to check in, before returning to other important activities, like tossing his grimy stuffed bear around, chewing his new rawhide bone, or napping. He knew. I considered trying again to let him sleep in my bed, for mutual comfort, but the snoring, farting, and cavorting were vivid in my memory and he was a good ten pounds heavier than the last time. I eighty-sixed the idea and he knew that too.

I saw myself becoming one of those old women in the supermarket checking the prices of soups for one. I thought of doing away with myself. But Libro bounded over and licked my ankles where the flannel nightgown ended, then my feet and I got perspective along with wet insteps.

His nose was against my skin, inhaling. His eyes, and the bone above them where there would have been eyebrows if he'd had them, were lifted. Had he done the trick? Was I okay? If I weren't here, who would mix the wet and dry food in exactly the right combination? Who had the gentle touch to stick Q-tips into his deep ears and not rupture anything? Who would teach him another language? Spanish, English, and dog were not enough; I was thinking of French next. I'd made a covenant to care for him and I intended to keep it.

Living with Libro went a long way toward making self-pity impossible. We romped in the park in the cold, me in my sweats, long underwear, and gloves with some fingers free, so I could leash and unleash him without fumbling. I bought a blue Frisbee, which I tossed and he caught. He flung it to the ground and stomped on it or held it clamped in his mouth, racing away in impish delight. When Josie, Mattie, Zooey, or any other dog tried to take the Frisbee away, Libro let them. Material things still meant little to him. The sacred quality of his home aside, he was willing to share or not to care.

Over the River
and through the Woods

....

Like everyone else at holiday time, we went visiting. Before we set out for lunch with my dear friend, a rich, famous lady who lived on Madison Avenue, I gave him a long bath in citrus shampoo, a rigorous tooth-cleaning, and a little talking-to about manners. Except for our Fifth Avenue stroll and the prowl in the Armani boutique some months back, Libro probably didn't know much about life on the east side, where some dogs wore Fendi and Gucci and behaved with gentility. He'd have to watch his ruffian ways.

The lady sent her car. Libro sat politely beside me on the backseat. To forestall accidents, we walked around the block once before approaching the canopied entry.

Inside, chandeliers hung from the ceiling and two sweeping staircases stood like angels' wings on either side of a glittering Christmas tree. Libro was very excited. The discreetly smiling uniformed doorman held the door. We rushed in. There really is no sound quite like doggy nails on a marble floor.

The elevator man bowed slightly, nodded, and held the gate open. Libro entered with élan and managed to stay off the purple upholstered seat within, although he sniffed every corner of the interior, which looked like Lily Langtry's boudoir, as it rose several floors.

We entered directly into the lady's living room, where the maid had us wait. I accompanied Libro on a brief and very controlled tour of the room, then settled myself on the brocade-covered sofa with Libro "down" on the soft rug. We waited. The lady, as always, made an entrance, sweeping into the room in a stylish navy dress and heels, hair and makeup impeccable. Libro rose. I introduced them. She admired his collar and gave him a light, elegant caress, akin to an air kiss, atop his head, red fingernails sailing through the air. Because she called everybody "darling," she addressed him as "Libro, darling." He was in awe.

We eventually went in to lunch, the lady and I, starting with split pea soup, the maid's specialty, and gossip, ours. The lady, a great collector of "beaus," was always wise about the perfidy of men, which she advised simply ignoring. She *tsk-tsk-ed* as I told her about the last of Mickey. Libro, acclimated to his surroundings, was allowed to investigate the entire, enormous apartment. I had given my word he would behave. And he did, trotting down one long hallway, peeping into several guest bedrooms, oblivious to the fact that they had housed ambassador-darlings and other VIPs. He visited the kitchen, where the thoughtful maid had set a water bowl on the floor, and wandered, uneventfully, through the lady's bedroom, dressing room, and study until he came to rest back in the living room, under the grand piano, flat on the rug, chin on his paws.

The lady was impressed. Her piano is the heart and soul of her home, perhaps her life, these days, for she stands beside it every day, practicing, rehearsing, keeping her lovely voice in shape. As Libro lay there, watching us through the archway as we ate, talked, and laughed in the dining room, only a few steps away, I wondered, proudly, if I could use him to sniff out water in arid places or gold in the Sierra Madre.

After lunch, we went out and walked around the block, the lady in a fur-lined coat, myself in black wool, and Libro darling in his usual. His Lord Fauntleroy manners left him the minute he was back in a familiar habitat that, for all its east side trimmings, was still sidewalk, tree, buildings, and people. He became quite Brooklyn, pulling rudely to the right, lifting his leg to pee against a building, loping left, sniffing the base of a tree, then marking it. He tried to follow a young man laden with packages, but I held him back. He stopped, nearly tripping the lady, as a limousine drew up, the door opened, and an elderly couple emerged.

"No, Libro," I said, "it's not your car." As though he didn't know.

We made a complete rectangle: up to Park, where white lights on the traffic islands were coming on like a string of pearls draped from Ninety-sixth Street down to what I still call the PanAm building; right, then right again, down the side street, returning to the lady's building on Madison. She paused on the staircase and said, very gently, but in a distinct, Miss-Otis-Regrets way, "he's very nice, darling, but I really think he has to go to school."

I felt like someone had said my boyfriend had bad table manners or picked his nose, but the feeling passed as soon as we were back on home turf. He peed on the building at Riverside Drive, fooled around with the doorman, tried to visit the lobby, stared intensely toward Riverside Park as though the act of looking could transport him there. School, schmool, I thought. He was well enough educated and I wouldn't want to refine the dogness out of him, even if I could. What's the point of having a dog if he behaves like a preppy at some fancy lycée? He did, however, start going to a bar, which was more unnerving than school could have been.

THE BAR HAS ITS place in the local iconography. There is a bit of what the English call "town and gown" about my neighborhood, which is some ten blocks from Columbia University. The "gown" parts are those clearly catering to students and faculty—bookstores, once, but fewer now that on-line sellers had come along, stationery stores, fax and copy places, health food places, gourmet take-out, stores specializing in fifty-two styles of running shoes. The "town" parts were actually two different kinds—cafés and restaurants, video rental shops, D'Agostino's supermarkets and chain drug stores for the new gentry, who lived in renovated brownstones on the side streets or big prewar buildings on West End Avenue, and a dwindling number of bodegas, Laundromats, and coffeeshops frequented by Latinos, Blacks, and the white people who moved in when most apartments were rent-controlled.

The bar Libro fell in love with was the most "townie"

bar for blocks around. I'd never been inside it. I'm not much on bars, anyway, having spent many an hour watching Peter get bleary-eyed and hilarious in the company of strangers he never saw again and then crawl into bed with his pores oozing the smell of sour beer. Libro, apparently, felt otherwise.

We were passing by, as we often did en route to the newspaper stand or the bagel store. The bar's windows were sprayed with "Seasons Greetings" in pink, surrounded by gold glitter. Through the glass front door, Libro caught a glimpse of a long-haired white dog lying on the floor, gazing out. This was actually unusual. The city's rules, which seem to bend at an owner's whim, are that no dogs are allowed in places that sell food. This doesn't stop the corner grocers, who know they are competing for consumer dollars with lower-priced chain markets that strictly enforce the prohibition against animals. They need our business. The Armani boutique had allowed Libro in for entirely different reasons.

Whatever whim had turned the local bar into a "dog-friendly" place, it was good for Libro. He stopped to gaze in. The dog got to his feet and pressed his nose against the inner glass. Libro did the same from his side, then he lifted his paw and actually knocked on the door. He might have been trying to touch the other dog through the pane, but it looked to me like he was demanding entry. People on bar stools watched, laughed, and beckoned Libro inside. I was afraid he would break the door, with all the pounding, so we went in.

It wasn't much. Bottles against the wall, TV at each end, maybe a dozen bar stools, Formica tables, pool table, long, dark, wooden bar with a classic brass rail to lean your foot on. No vodka shots in Jell-O here. Most patrons had beer glasses or shot glasses in front of them. Locals, many of whom I recognized. And dog lovers. The white dog, who held Libro's attention for only a second, lived with a rangy dark man in a building near ours, and they had a green van that said "White Dog Moving" on the side. The only moving I ever saw was from one side of the street to another. It wasn't the dog that interested Libro; it was the bar.

A Willie Nelson tape was playing as Libro worked the smoky room. He stopped at every bar stool for scratches, rubs, and strokes. He would have gotten popcorn too, which sat in bowls on the bar, but I said no. I always feel like a killjoy in bars. Libro checked out the game at the pool table, expertly avoiding a beer glass sitting on the edge. The two men playing stopped good-naturedly while he sniffed, but did not move, the eight ball, perched almost on the lip of a middle pocket.

Then Libro walked confidently behind the bar, where a woman in jeans, with a blond ponytail, was setting up drinks. She didn't seem bothered or surprised to find him at her feet, trying to lick her leg. He sat. She put a drink in front of a customer, wiped her hands, and opened a drawer below the rows of bottles. Libro's tail whipped back and forth. She had a biscuit! Into his eager mouth it popped. Then she had another. And another. I was killjoy again, feeling compelled to say, enough, and to try to get him out of there.

"Libro, come!"

He didn't take his eyes off the bartender.

"Yo! Libro! *Venga!*"

The way he looked at the bartender would have put Dante and Beatrice to shame, he the awestruck admirer, she the perfect lady on the pedestal.

In no language would he respond. The guys at the pool table, one leaning into a bridge he'd made of his fingers on the green felt, the other standing with his cue stick at his side, like a soldier with his musket, were watching and laughing.

"*Usted habla español?*"

"No," I said, deflecting him, "but my doggy does."

The bartender broke the spell herself, bringing me a biscuit and telling Libro that if he left with his "mommy," he could have it. I swallowed my objection to *mommy* and led him outside to a chorus, of "bye," and, "*adios*, Libro," from the people in the bar.

In spite of my distaste for the place and for seedy dives in general, the event had its own kind of charm. It was also a clue to Libro's past, which still bedeviled me. I had pieced together, at that point, that he'd been in a good home (he was too friendly to have been abused with any consistency), probably with a black man if not a black family (from the way he responded to black people in the street), and some trauma had led to his maiming and abandonment. I had, in the first weeks, walked him around uptown streets to see if he recognized people or places, but the minute he became "mine," I stopped, lest I lose him.

Unlike the Armani boutique, bars were apparently familiar turf to Libro. Unlike the country, which interested but did not delight him, the bar—particularly, I'm willing to hazard, the smell of the bar—was close to his idea of heaven. I say this because, after that first time, he became obsessed. We could no longer pass by, especially on a Saturday night, when the ponytailed bartender was at work, without his head-lowering, neck-stretched pull toward the place, followed by his pounding on the door, racing inside, schmoozing, and sitting for biscuits. He didn't understand at all that bars are not open at nine in the morning. When people on Broadway, heading for work, saw him dragging me toward the glass door, I laughed and said, "he's an alcoholic," with a what-can-you-do-about-it shrug of my shoulders.

He wanted to be a regular. I didn't. Some nights, I waited outside in the cold while he made his rounds, thinking, How did I end up trailing after yet another male with a bar problem?

I consulted the dog people, who still congregated, but for shorter periods of time, in the run. A few, including the couple with the fat white bulldogs who had been so imaginatively decked out for Halloween, said their dogs liked bars, even that bar, but they did too. Most had never been inside, never noticed the place; nor had their dogs. The petite lawyer who lives with an eleven-year-old mutt named Barclay had an opposite experience: for more than a year after he was adopted, when she and her husband opened a wine bottle, the dog ran to the other end of the apartment and cowered. It wasn't, she assured me, the sound of the cork popping, but the smell of the wine. I didn't bother asking Clarence about himself and Lola, or the mystery writer and his wife about Josie. They were so emphatically not bar types, any of them, although I could see Lola at someplace like Windows on the World, staring out the huge panes at some prey in the sky. I tried talking to Jennifer, but all she could tell me was that her husband had disappeared on another bender and she thought he probably wouldn't be back until after New Year's and would I keep an eye out for him when Libro was prowling the bars?

Libro became a regular. Hello, Libro, they'd say as he charged through the door, *Hóla*, Libro. There were often other dogs in the bar, including the White Dog Moving dog and the bulldogs, but he paid them no mind. It was the atmosphere of beer and cigarette smoke, the pool table, the bartender, the biscuit drawer, and the patrons he cared about. They all knew his story—I'd dutifully answered the doggy questions about his age and background, and every time somebody came in who hadn't met him, I'd answer again.

One night a man who said his name was Jesús was discussing with me the aftermath of Libro's terror in the streets. Libro was up on his hind legs entertaining customers from behind the bar while his adored bartender poured.

"Bet he eats his food too fast, huh?" Jesús said.

"Wolfs it down," I answered. "How did you know?"

"Comes from being on the street," he said. "They get frantic. People who live on the street do the same thing."

Feliz Navidad

....

I think of myself as a rational person, a materialist in the sense of believing in things I can see, touch, smell, hear, and feel. I remain skeptical about everything else, although the spiritual and the mystical had come knocking on my door quite loudly all year. I dated the intrusion of the inexplicable from the moment I took Libro home with me, an act so out of character that it was, at the time, irrational. So maybe you could say I took the encounter with Jesús in the bar as a sign that sent me out into the streets with Libro on Christmas Eve in the uncorrupted spirit of the season.

"Let's go find lonely people to cheer up," I said. He

jumped up, anticipating, I'm sure, his regular nightly walk. It was late and light snow had been falling for an hour or two. The building was quiet. The boys had all gone back west for the holiday; Sophia and Ted were out; Lisa was singing at a church service. When he stepped out into the falling snow, Libro shook himself, to get the moisture off, but also put his nose to the ground and then into the air to investigate the thing that was clearly not rain. He stuck his tongue out, catching a snowflake. Where were you last winter? I wondered.

Faint white lines edged the black wrought iron fences along the street and there were sugary traces on the parked cars, but no accumulation on the ground. We turned left at Broadway, uptown, away from the seedy bar. Straus Park was empty. The liquor store, the Laundromat, and the chicken take-out place were closed. Libro trotted along with his head up, ears bouncing, an occasional flake settling on his dark coat and disappearing.

At 110th Street, the Christmas tree seller stood all alone, sipping coffee from a paper cup and guarding his last half-dozen pines and spruces. Libro loped up. The young man stooped down, smiling, to pet him. Libro boxed him. I let go of the leash and the two roughed it up. Libro picked up the dragging leash and gave it to the man to tug. While they pulled and growled, the seller said he was determined to stay out until the last tree was sold, then head home to Canada. He'd been in the same spot for more than twelve hours.

So I gave him Libro for a little recreation. While I watched the trees, they ran around the block, disappearing into the darkness. Libro leaped in the air every few steps. Nobody came by. Man and dog reappeared around the corner, breathing heavily. A tree was offered, but I refused. I did take some cut branches.

Libro looked back, tail wagging, until the trees were out of sight and we were in front of the West End Bar, a Columbia landmark, where Allen Ginsberg once sat over a sheaf of poems. A panhandler stood out front, cup in one hand, piece of pastry in the other. Libro did his thing.

"Wow," the man said, "friendly dog."

"Yes. Merry Christmas."

"Ya know, ma'am, most dogs bark at me."

"Not this one."

I told him about Libro and black men and my thoughts about the back story. The man leaned over and tried to feed a piece of his pastry to the dog, whom he called "boy," but I stopped him. I remained prim on the subject of junk food. Besides, I thought the man deserved his whole gooey treat on Christmas Eve.

On our way back downtown, we met a woman in a wheelchair, with a blanket over her knees, alone in the street. Her eyes narrowed as Libro approached. I said he was friendly. She looked like she didn't believe me and I was prepared to keep going, but Libro pulled on his leash and sat down at her feet. She said she guessed maybe he was friendly and wheeled closer, putting her hand out to pat his head. He licked her hand. I said I was hoping to train him to work with people in hospitals and that he already knew not to jump on the chair. She turned her hand over so he could lick the palm.

"Boy or girl?"

"Boy." Year and a half, maybe. Rescued. Limps. Speaks Spanish. I gave her the whole litany.

"Think he'd like a ride on my lap?"

I thought she had a bottle under the blanket.

"Maybe. Libro, up!"

He rose from the ground.

"Up!" I said, again, but he didn't move. It's hard to explain to a dog that under some circumstances, the forbidden thing—like jumping up on a person in a wheelchair—is temporarily okay. She showed him it was. Looking back at me several times for reassurance, he got gingerly up into her lap.

"Take him for a ride if you want," I said. "He'd like that."

She looked disbelieving again, but rolled her chair away, one-handed, holding Libro around his middle with her other hand. He didn't look back. She rolled to the corner, spun the chair around, and came back. Libro climbed down a little less carefully.

"I think he really liked that," she said.

"He did. I'm sure he did. He's never had a ride in a wheelchair before."

"Merry Christmas."

"*Feliz Navidad.*"

"You're amazing," I said to him as we walked away. "You get these beautiful branches, you meet a panhandler who not only doesn't ask for money, but tries to give you a present, and you cheer a lady in a wheelchair by riding in her lap." Libro was licking the snow, thicker now, on the ground and didn't seem to care how amazing he was.

As we walked through Straus Park, I saw something glistening on a dark bench. Libro sniffed and I looked. Lying there were three yellow roses, still in florist's cellophane, tied with a ribbon, aglow like gold in the snow. Forgotten? Cast away by a petulant sweetheart? The place was silent and empty, no traces, no footsteps. I picked the flowers up, cradling them with the pine branches.

EARLY THE NEXT MORNING, we went out in the snow. I had dreamed for months of Libro cavorting in a white-carpeted field and cavort he did, along with Josie, Barclay, a husky named Q, who was entirely in his element, and Megan, a dingolike dog who had lost her tail to a car accident. As we turned to leave the park, I noticed Libro's feet, which seemed to be bleeding. "Ohmygod," I screamed. Benjamin, who lives with Megan, ran over. Libro, worried, was licking my leg, covered in long johns, sweats, and thick, high boots.

"His paws. He's bleeding."

I leaned over and lifted one. Benjamin laughed. Libro's paw was bright pink, but not from blood. The grime was gone, washed off by the snow, cleaner than it had been after a bath or even a swim. The bottoms of Megan's paws were the same.

Okay, fine, then, I was still an idiot who lived with a magical spirit masquerading as a dog in what could start out as a Frank Capra movie but turn on a dime into something Woody Allen would have made.

Later, the snow stopped and the sky turned bright silver. A bunch of teal helium balloons were caught in a bare tree on the Drive. Libro wandered from stone wall to curb more lackadaisically than usual. I couldn't remember when I'd felt so at peace. But a woman in a down coat walking a mangy poodle didn't seem to share the mood.

"Put that dog on a leash," she snarled as we approached.

"Don't worry," I said.

The woman, infected with misery, snarled again.

"It's Christmas," I reminded her. "And he's friendly."

"But *I'm* not," she said.

"So maybe we should put *you* on a leash."

Libro and I ran away, hurtling along Riverside Drive. I felt like an eight-year-old boy who had just tossed a snowball at a girl. I don't know what Libro felt like, but from the looks of him—pumpernickel streak leaving paw prints in the snow—it was pretty good.

Sweethearts

....

I was never big on Valentine's Day, bringing, as it does, a high schoolish anxiety about how popular I might or might not be. Where I come from, how many cards you got was more important than who they were from. As a presumed adult, deep in a romance, I'd scoffed at the conventional flowers and candy—roses made me sneeze and I'd had my fill of chocolate by the time I was eleven. Diamonds would have been okay, but then, diamonds are okay any day of the year.

This year, February 14 would be especially hard. It was my parents' anniversary date and with my mother less than a year in her grave, my father would be suffering in ways I could only imagine and never assauage. My own loss—of Mickey and the possibilities I'd entertained—had come back in dreams full of longing. Without much choice in the matter, I decided to do what I could for my grieving father and ignore the rest of the day.

Libro and I took our morning walk. On the way out of the park, we saw Matty, the male Portie, and Alice, the younger of his two "mommies." We stopped. While Libro and Matty circled and sniffed each other, Alice handed me something wrapped in red tissue paper. A valentine for Libro.

At home, I unwrapped the paper. Inside was something that looked like a cloven hoof, gray and hard. I handed it over to a tail-wagging, high-jumping Libro, who chomped and batted it around for a while, then left it on the kitchen floor near his bowls, along with his collection of half-chewed rawhide bones. Like me, he delighted in the getting of gifts, not the things themselves, which quickly lost their appeal. He wasn't a gold digger.

Now I had to go shopping. People give you gifts, you respond. Although I had other plans for the day, Libro and I went out again, up to Broadway, where pails of brilliant red and pink roses were for sale outside the Korean grocery. We crossed the street and went into the pet store. Libro tried to snare a smelly elephant's ear, but I put it back. He grabbed a biscuit out of the bin.

At the counter, a woman was buying a heart-shaped cookie for her black, red-sweater-clad pug, who looked like he'd rather be in Barbados.

We took the flavored rawhide bone I'd chosen into the stationery store on the corner and I asked them to gift wrap it. I never felt so stupid in my life. I also bought a card, from a rack full of floral designs, smiley faces, and Victorian calligraphy. This one had a dog on it, cocking his head in a terminally cute pose. I stuck the card in my pocket.

At Matty's building, two blocks away, I gave the package to the doorman, over Libro's irate objections. The doorman acted accustomed to receiving things for the dogs in the building.

"Is that Matty's girlfriend?" the young uniformed man asked, smiling at Libro, whose eyes were still fixed on the package.

"No. He's a boy."

The doorman was calculating. His thinking was visible:

First he thought, Oops, and his eyebrows went up.

Then he thought, Well, Matty lives with two women, so why not, and his mouth pursed.

"That's okay too," he said, turning what he clearly believed to be a tolerant smile on Libro, who thought he was about to get the gift-wrapped package and licked the doorman's trouser leg.

Then we walked along Broadway to the bar, an act of complete capitulation on my part.

Although the bartender seemed like a nice woman, I didn't approve of Libro's relationship with her, of his obsession with beery smells and bars. Nonetheless, he was smitten and who was I to deny a crazy passion? He'd given up on Lola's aloofness and Josie's ambivalence. He deserved a little extracurricular romance, and the bartender, for her appreciation of Libro, not to mention the hundreds of biscuits, deserved a valentine.

It was a little past noon and Libro's girlfriend was only on at night. Two men sat alone at opposite ends of the bar. Libro looked for his beloved under the pool table, under the door to the ladies' room, and then the men's room and behide the bar, where a burly man I'd never seen was laughing. We left the card. Libro refused to go, hunching down on the floor and looking at me smugly, defiantly. The TV showed a weather report: cold and gray.

"Come home with me and I'll give you a biscuit, sweetheart," I said.

He responded to the word *biscuit*.

At home, I called my dad, listening with teary eyes to his stoical description of how hard it was to avoid the fact that this was Valentine's Day. You couldn't go to the the supermarket without encountering mountainous displays of candy and flowers; you couldn't drive any road without passing flower stands and rose-sellers.

If you had a dog, I thought, it would be even worse.

Warm

Crackdown

....

The first signs of trouble came with the first warming days. The city turned mean. Every month, a different part of the population was under attack. As part of a cleanup, crackdown, or just plain hissy fit, the mayor declared war on squeegee men ("get rid of 'em"), then sidewalk peddlers (too much shish kebab was choking Manhattan), and then cabdrivers. The targets were marginal groups, not masters of the universe or super-models, although the latter too were in a state of some agitation about their working conditions. The local evening news showed people protesting and being led off to jail.

Libro ignored the evening news because he ignored the television set, whose images were far too two-dimensional to engage him. Likewise, he'd ignored my efforts to interest him in his own face in a mirror, proving once again that dogs are nothing like babies. He knew that television was not real—when a dog barked in a TV show, Libro, who was able to hear me hit the "save" key on my computer keyboard (work was over, we were going out), ignored it.

He knew little about politics, although he'd been used as a prop in the November senatorial campaign, when I pinned a button touting our candidate to his collar and took him to work the subway station entrance at Broadway and 103rd Street. Harried people eager to get home were nonetheless unable to resist petting him and thereby getting a piece of the candidate's literature slapped into their hands. Our man won.

He retained his affection for police, still sniffing the pants legs of every street cop and jumping up to the windows of parked patrol cars. Whether the police genuinely liked him, were improving community relations, or were simply expressing gratitude for having a fan, I couldn't tell. After a series of police shootings of unarmed young men, they needed all the fans they could get.

So Libro was happy to see *Law and Order* being taped

a block away. He peed on a patrol car, sniffed the cables, and made eyes at the crew. Jerry Ohrbach, who plays a lead detective in the show, sat in a high canvas chair, his hair looking very dark and his makeup a little orange. My savvy neighbors, crowded together on the sidewalk, left the star alone. Not Libro.

He ambled over and sat at Ohrbach's feet. I, attached to Libro's leash, had no choice but to follow. The actor was gracious. I answered the usual polite questions:

"Libro."

"He's almost two."

But couldn't stop there, urging Libro to demonstrate his bilingual talents.

"*Siéntate*," I said, but he was already sitting.

I went into stage mother overdrive. His eyes. His story. His discipline. Surely there was a walk-on role for the dog in this episode. Ohrbach looked away, exactly the way Libro does when what I'm saying annoys him.

THE MEAN SPRING FELT a shade meaner a few nights later, when police cars with lights flashing were forcing traffic into a single lane on Riverside Drive. Cars were stopped, drivers questioned. It looked like Checkpoint Charlie. He must have thought this was another television show. He pulled forward ready to say hello.

"Excuse me," I said, while Libro wagged his tail wildly and sniffed one cop's leg, "what's going on?"

They were checking for stolen cars. When I asked why only black drivers were being stopped, the cop heaved an exasperated sigh.

"Lady," he said, "don't you own a car?"

I yanked Libro away. He kept looking back longingly at the cops and the lights. The cops were his friends and he was still looking for the camera.

SOON AFTER THAT, a sour magazine article about "mad dogs" appeared, written by a former comedy writer for *Saturday Night Live* whose humor had deserted him. He didn't like the doggy poop in Riverside Park, the animals chasing around without their leashes, the crushed grass. His solution: everybody should keep their dogs in their country houses and out of the city altogether.

I read the article right after I'd read a dozen garden catalogs, dreaming of clematis for summer and lamenting that it was too late to plant bulbs. It ruined my mood.

"Well, Libro," I said, "You animal. You're ruining the park."

He rolled over on his back and I rubbed his belly, brushing his "sweet spot," the raised scar remaining from the surgery that had neutered him. His legs spasmed with

pleasure, his face looked transported, ecstatic, even or-
gasmic. I'd stopped doing this in public because people in
the park or on the sidewalk raised their eyebrows and either smiled or looked deliberately away, apparently as-
suming the pleasure they witnessed was sexual when it
was only pleasure.

"So," I added, "seems we need a country house pronto.
So we can be isolated and I can get lost in the woods and
creepy crawly things can invade my dreams. You could
hunt and kill." In the privacy of his own, albeit rented
and urban, home, he wanted more rubbing. I obliged.

The majority of people who frequented the park with
their dogs hadn't read the article and didn't care. They
just wanted to be left alone. Those who were offended or
annoyed differed about what to do. Ignore it, some said,
lay low and it will go away. Fight back, said others. Write
letters. Point out the damage done by soccer players,
touch-footballers, and volleyball bangers trampling the
grass, digging up the ground in their enthusiasm. De-
scribe the debris humans leave, the fried chicken boxes,
soda cans, and slime. Point out that our community has
made the park safer, being there at odd hours. Call the
magazine. Do we want a park or a grass museum?

I held my tongue and put down my pen, joining the
wait- and-see contingent.

A few days later, on a cool morning, the trees were beginning to bud and volunteers were turning over the
ground in the community garden. More joggers and squirrels than we'd seen in a while were scampering around in
the park. Libro was fooling with Amber, a mutt who held
a ball in her mouth, trying to lick Libro without dropping
the ball. Matthew the photographer, Amber's owner, was
encased in a Walkman and I was laughing.

A green truck pulled up at the base of the hill where
we were cavorting and two workmen began unloading
bales of wire fencing. While Amber guarded her ball,
Matthew and I and Libro watched. By the time Libro decided to investigate, the men had driven stakes into the
ground and were unrolling a length of wire fencing. His
tags sounded like chimes as he raced toward the action,
alarming one of the workers.

"He's okay," I shouted, "he's friendly."

The man motioned for me to come nearer. Libro
sniffed the fence and sat at the worker's feet, turning on
the charm. His tail wiggled. He made eye contact. His
forehead lifted.

For once, charm failed. The hill, we were told, was
now off-limits to dogs. No discussion. The worker was
only carrying out orders. Whose he did not say. We were
directed to the fenced-in dog run.

It turned out that Libro and I had been living in a fool's paradise. Our outdoor frolicking had been at the forbearance of the Parks Department, which had an unofficial policy of allowing dogs to go free early in the morning and late at night. The official laws of the city said that dogs had to be on leashes everywhere. Frederick Law Olmsted, who designed both Central Park and Riverside Park in the nineteenth century, made a special point of excluding canines from enjoying them. The dogs he had in mind, I'm sure, were wild, predatory beasts, a health hazard, not the highly socialized, tagged, rabies-inoculated apartment-dwellers of the twenty-first century, many of whom had human entourages—vets, trainers, walkers, groomers—larger than Olmsted's. The Victorian ladies with lapdogs, I suppose, were not barred, nor did they walk their dogs themselves.

I'd been a reasonably good citizen, holding Libro's leash in our civilized world—along Broadway or West End Avenue, in the teller's line at the bank, in the drugstore, the market, the magazine store. But the park was a different story. He was well trained and sweet tempered, gentle with little dogs and old people. He never tried to eat a child or run off to join the foreign legion. He feared moving cars and didn't chase or dart around them. Wandering without a leash in the park, the only harm he'd done had been to himself, from ingesting pieces of fried chicken careless people left on the ground, or human feces, which lurked in lumps along the park wall.

Once, right after a bad afternoon rainstorm, we'd raced into the park, the only person and dog there. The air was as fresh as any mountain village and the trees dripped what tasted like spring water as we passed beneath them. If we did those things now, as the crackdown got underway, if we dashed along without a nylon cord binding us to each other, we'd be outlaws.

A white van started riding back and forth from sunup 'til after sundown, stopping to issue $100 tickets to any human whose canine was unfettered. City cops on horseback joined the hunt, leaving huge piles of horse dung on the paths, which strongly attracted the dogs. A black sedan belonging to the sanitation police cruised Riverside Drive.

The fenced-in dog run was now so crowded it looked like a subway car at the height of rush hour. Rottweilers pushed against chows and stepped over terriers. Humans filled the three small benches and cutoff tree stumps. Nobody played ball or spun a Frisbee. The possibility of a fight, human or canine, hovered. The wrong kind of look, an unintended nudge, anything could set it off. Expecting dogs to have fun in such cramped quarters was as bizarre as asking a couple in evening dress to waltz in a telephone booth.

Word drifted around among the dog people crowded into the run that Ms. X had received a $200 ticket, Mr. Y a $400 summons. People gave false names to the sanitation police or ran away when stopped. A woman had been followed out of the park, to the bagel store and the laundry, by police trying to see where she and her Akita lived. I walked warily, expecting little men to leap from behind tree trunks, shouting "aha!" like Peter Sellers in *Lolita*. The dogs were being driven nuts by tense humans who let them play, reined them in, released them again, and looked over their shoulders all the time. People were being driven nuts too.

The dog people, many of whom would have shuddered at any other kind of civil disobedience, formed an underground. The dogs needed exercise and they couldn't get it in the cramped dog run, so humans risked tickets and got up a signal system to warn of the presence of "authorities." "They're four blocks away," someone would whisper, exiting the park. Or, "They just left." Everyone not playing with a dog was a potential informer and we congregated in small, edgy groups, suspicious of anyone we didn't know.

It wasn't the French Resistance. We weren't defending

the Warsaw Ghetto. Riverside Park was not a border crossing patrolled by *La Migra*. From the way people were talking, myself included, the nature of the struggle was not always clear. A few people muttered "Fascists" when the white van appeared. Tony, who still lugged his oxygen tank, insisted "the oppressed" had to organize. A museum curator out with his husky bragged he'd be willing to pay a hundred dollars for his dog to have fun. A woman with a black mutt whispered, when he left, that the curator's attitude was dividing us along class lines.

Old-timers said it had happened before, a cycle of crackdowns and let-ups driven by nobody knew what. Why now, I wondered. Millennial anxiety? The malling of New York? These were conservative times. We lived in an atmosphere of containment, a preference for the straight-laced, buttoned-up, clean-cut, and an aversion to wildness and excess. Libro and friends at play in the park were wanton, unpredictable. I had come to relish the way they lay on the ground wrassling or stood on hind legs and embraced. I wished I could do the same.

Women who run with the wolves, indeed. Not in this town. The dogs chased, stopped, waiting for the signal only they could perceive, whooshed off again. I envied their ability to understand each other. Libro was especially talented at organizing a chain of dogs with himself at the front, racing up and down like a souped-up conga line.

While the reigning-in of such shenanigans made life difficult, I hadn't counted on how quickly a stigma can grow. Passersby who had once smiled indulgently or even appreciatively at frolicking dogs scowled and looked away. Many avoided us altogether. A few weeks into the crackdown, the rumor mill in the park spit out a terrifying tale. A woman had been walking her poodle on Broadway. The dog picked up something in its mouth at 106th Street. Two blocks later, he died on the sidewalk.

I WAS AFRAID.

I found out through Cedric that there was something to fear. Cedric had become an entrepreneur. His wares, artfully arranged on a blanket in front of the D'Agostino's market at 110th Street and Broadway, included stained paperback books, several pairs of beaten up shoes, a cracked vase, some tarnished spoons, a clock, and a tape recorder.

"Yo! Libro!"

I scanned the book titles while Cedric, declaring he had something for Libro, dug around in a large green trash bag.

"It's in here, boy. Wait. I been savin' it for you."

All Libro wanted was to play with Cedric. Eventually, the treasure hunt in the trash bag was suspended and Libro got his way.

"Such great animals," Cedric said, rubbing Libro behind the ears and leaning over for a sloppy kiss. "Why would anybody want to kill a dog?"

"Who wants to kill a dog?"

He looked at me with bloodshot eyes.

"The guy who put poison in chicken and put it out on Broadway. Down there." He pointed south.

"You know who it was?"

"Guy hangs out in the park. You seen him. He been laughin' about it."

I imagined calling the precinct:

"I want to report a murder."

"Who is the victim?"

"A poodle."

"I see. And the suspect?"

"Well, I don't know his name. But there's a guy named Cedric who the murderer confessed to."

"Last name and address for this Cedric?"

"Don't know his name. You can find him in Riverside Park, past a hundred and eighth Street, third bench from the end."

"Right."

THE DOG PEOPLE ALL over the city organized to fight back. Given that our neighborhood is full of veterans of the civil rights movement, the women's movement, SDS, and Act-Up, I was amazed to see who among the locals stepped forward. Clarence, most of all. Diffident and haughty as he had seemed to me, he proved hard working and smart as an organizer. He had signs printed for the dog run, telling people how to sign up. He formed committees, took a group to survey canine situations in other neighborhoods, looked into ways to use computer technology to keep us all in touch. Most days now, he walked Lola in the park with her leash in one hand and a clipboard in the other.

An observer would have been hard-pressed to say what the several hundred souls gathered weeks later in a Broadway church had in common. Aging preppies with briefcases sat beside young men in dreadlocks; gay partners and lesbian couples held hands; tough macho guys whispered with upper east side ladies in stockings and heels; several women alone with young children tried to keep them occupied. These were the joint forces of people with dogs. I was almost afraid Mickey would show up, but he didn't.

We listened politely to speeches about "being positive" and "staying on message" and using diplomacy. A few exasperated middle-aged hippies jumped up to wave their arms wildly and urge a doggy march on city hall and a shutdown of traffic. They were contained by the more civilized majority.

"Listen, Libro," I said, when I got home. I told him I'd been on many barricades and I was surely no coward in the unpopular opinions department, but I'd also been a jogger in the park tripping on dogs, and I had a life, including making a living to keep him in dog biscuits. I couldn't support canine anarchy.

"I'm gonna watch your back like you watch mine," I said, "but *La Passionaria de los Perros* I will not become. Let's get on with our lives."

Revelations

· · · · · · · · · · · · ·

I was still worried about Libro's leg. I'd collected suggestions for regular doctors, doggy orthopedists, and holistic
healers we should see, some as far away as Chicago. I settled for a more local referral, a vet who used acupuncture
as well as traditional medicine. We walked there.

Libro misbehaved right away, wandering around the
waiting room, sniffing out the doggy treats, and trying to
see the doctor before the doctor was ready to see him.
Libro understood the difference between what you can
expect at a clinic (he'd been very obedient at the
ASPCA) and in a private practice. Or I did.

He climbed on the scale and sent the needle up close

to fifty pounds. He got a battery of shots, including some I'd never heard of and one for kennel cough, which would allow him to go stay in a doggy day-care facility. I was obviously in this for the long haul.

The handsome Dr. Raclyn, who sometimes appears in magazine ads for the Mac PowerBook, felt the right hind leg, while Libro searched his face. His spindly leg was much thicker now, with a pronounced thigh muscle. His limp was only erratic. He ran like the wind. I considered his healing a tribute to the community of care he had collected around himself, the boys next door, Cedric and his crew, Lisa, Clarence, the doormen, Sophia and Ted, Rosemary, Diana, the park people, even the barflies, and to his own spunky spirit.

When Dr. Raclyn pressed his knee joint, Libro flinched and pulled his leg away. We weren't out of the woods yet.

An X ray was in order.

The doctor and an assistant led Libro away, to a back room. He went along without looking back. If he didn't lie still on the table, he'd be put to sleep for a while, for the sake of a clear picture. I was not allowed to stay with him—but I could get him to lie still!—in fact, I should leave and return in two hours.

I thought I'd read for a while at the Barnes and Noble store, the neighborhood's unofficial library. There was nothing much new in women's studies and I wasn't in a biography mood, so I found myself running my fingers along the titles in the "Animals and the Environment" section. Strange, I thought, for a writer not to read a book for information. Haven't had to, I answered myself, life and Libro have taught you what you need to know about him.

I carried some volumes to a table near "Self Help" and sat down in an empty chair. When I looked up, an hour had passed. Boxers, I had learned, are descended from the old fighting dogs of Tibet and were "perfected" as a breed in Germany. I couldn't begin to imagine what that meant. They are thought of as the philosophers of the dog world, because of the faraway looks in their eyes, the sense that they are thinking deep thoughts.

"Balderdash," said I. "The worst kind of anthropomorphizing."

I'd read on: "fighters with sentimental hearts . . . impish, with great senses of humor . . . a playfulness that persists into old age."

Not bad.

"Courageous and affectionate."

Sure.

"Legendary alertness."

You bet.

"A special regard for humans understood to be help-less or handicapped; a deep sense of community respon-sibility."

Something was making me uneasy.

"A jaunty self-assurance. Easily bored. Needs a lot of attention and involvement from the owner."

I'd pushed the books away and was sitting staring off into space, probably appearing philosophical to an observer. Actually, I was feeling a little disappointed. Almost every description fit Libro exactly. Were these breed characteristics like horoscopes, where you could read your own situation into predictions for any sign of the zodiac? I suspected not. Everything so unique to Libro appeared to be genetic, bred in. Every sui generis corner of his personality. Impossible! *No me digas!*

Far more disconcerting, however, was this: I too have been called alert, playful, sentimental, and impish. I have a deep sense of community. I am easily bored. Oh, dear. I do like to be alerted when the uncanny is about to de-scend on me.

I found myself on Broadway in a daze, walking in and out of stores. I looked at ocean liner dinnerware in the Fish's Eddy store, linen garment bags and cedar blocks at Hold Everything. I fondled lipsticks at Cosmetics Plus, then checked my watch.

We were a perfect match, Libro and I. If I'd been thinking about getting a dog, if I'd filled in a questionnaire
about my personality and been paired with the right
breed, it would have been a boxer. It would have been
Libro. But I hadn't chosen him, hadn't been looking. I
wanted to call someone, but couldn't think who. And the
two hours were up.

I waited in the vet's reception area while an assistant
brought Libro out on his leash. He pulled away from her
and raced into my arms.

"We belong together," I whispered. It was really all too
tacky for me.

He'd behaved well, the assistant said, except for trying
to go after a cat who was waiting for a minor surgery.
Good boy.

Dr. Raclyn came out, looking solemn.

"I think you're going to be very surprised," he said.

We went into the examining room, where I told Libro
to *siéntate* and the vet pointed to the X ray clipped to a
light box.

On Libro's dark hind leg, running thigh to knee to an-
kle, was a bright mercury-colored line, like a frozen river.

There were two steel rods in that leg.

"That's pretty expensive surgery," the vet said.

I gasped.

"You didn't know?"

I didn't know.

The picture looked like a piece of modern sculpture, an Arp perhaps, simple, bright, metallic, geometric, surgical pin, rod, pin, rod, and pin again.

I touched Libro's right hind leg, feeling nothing.

The leg had been smashed, presumably by a car, and rebuilt with awesome precision. Before he was a year old, then, before we found each other, Libro had been hurt and cared for, hospitalized, anesthetized, medicated, and rehabilitated. The truth was entirely the opposite of my grim fiction about his past: he'd not been beaten and broken by a human devil at all, but profoundly loved.

It made sense: Libro's apprehension around traffic, his rapid way of crossing a street, his geniality, his beautiful collar and good manners. But the news also reopened the mystery: who was his guardian angel and what had happened? A theft, most likely, or a death.

The vet was talking about medication for his stiff joints and I was cradling the upper third of Libro in my lap.

"What happened to you?" I said into his amber eyes. I'd never wished more passionately that he could speak.

Walking home through Riverside Park, where trees were already in bud and volunteers were setting scarlet flowered plants into the ground, I couldn't keep my eyes off his leg or shake the imprint on my retina of that steely picture. He was scampering, rushing up to birds nibbling bread crumbs, looking amazed when they flew away, but I was lost in the *clank clank clank* of the steel only I could hear.

A survivor.

Happy Birthday

....

By late May, Libro's leg was more flexible and he could sit in a nearly normal position. I made peace with knowing he would always have something of a Chaplinesque limp. He'd always been at peace with it.

Memorial Day weekend, I decided, was Libro's birthday. He was now more or less two years old. That Friday, we set out for the park, where the courtesy of off-leash play before nine in the morning had been restored. The dog owners groups claimed victory, but the cynics said that Parks Department personnel had been shifted to the beaches for the summer season. They'd be back.

We ran into Enrique and Paco again. Enrique had the beginnings of a mustache and looked about five years older, but was still on his roller blades. Paco seemed withdrawn or stoned.

"*Holá*, Libro!"

It was as though they had seen him yesterday. He licked their faces, tail wagging ferociously. When Enrique took Libro's leash and skated away, the dog looked deliriously happy, but when Enrique stopped and tried to get Libro to pull him along, he refused. They came back and Paco took his turn.

"*Tira*, Libro," pull, he said, with some anger.

Libro sat down on the grass. Paco yanked his leash.

"Leave him alone," I said. "He doesn't want to pull you."

We met the morning crew. "His leg looks much better," people said, watching him speed after Josie, Mattie, or his newest pal, Zeus, a lumbering Swiss mountain dog. Lola, on hiatus from her life in dog shows, still paid Libro no mind, but her new kid brother, whom Clarence had named Shag, snarled at any dog that came near. Libro ran longer and harder than he ever had and collapsed in a tongue-hanging pant at my feet. I no longer thought this signaled a heart attack.

It was a cloudy, humid day, with rain threatening. Close to nine, we left the park, went up the steps, along the virtually traffic-free Drive, onto our street, past the new doorman at the corner. The one with the El Greco face had been fired for spending too much time hanging out in the street.

Phoenix was toddling along with her father and when she saw us turn the corner, she ran toward us, arms flapping, screeching "Wibwo."

"*Siéntate*," I told him as she approached. "And no jumping."

I forgot to say no kissing.

Libro's slobber brought tears to her face and she sat down on the sidewalk to weep, which only made Libro want to kiss her more. I restrained him. Phoenix's father laughed and lifted her into his consoling arms.

"Tell Libro no," I said to Phoenix. She buried her head in her father's shoulder and murmured "no." I repeated: "If you don't like what he's doing, say no to him, very loud." I never felt like Nancy Reagan before.

Her skeptical face peered down at the dog.

"*No*," she said.

He look up at her, balefully.

"Tell him to sit."

"Sit," she said, from the safety of her father's arms.

He sat.

• • •

UPSTAIRS, I BREWED COFFEE and took my vitamin C, E, A&D, antioxidants, and antihistamines. Then I fed Libro his medications, a capsule of pain-killing Rimadyl stuck into the back of his throat, a glucosamine tablet ground into his new combination of wet and dry dog food, along with some oily drops to prevent dry skin. What a pair.

The old white plastic bowls had been replaced by green Fiestaware. If the food wasn't mixed exactly to his liking, or the tablet not entirely dissolved, Libro backed off, looked at me, and barked. I'd learned well; I did it right this time and he was chomping away. Remember, I said, when you were so grateful to have a home that you did everything anybody asked of you and you loved everything I gave you and did for you? And now you want your food done just so and you don't want Paco and Enrique to treat you like a husky. How come you suddenly have so many opinions? Is this self-esteem? Have you come to believe that what you want matters?

He wasn't listening because he'd become a stalker, following a big dark brown roach that skittered across the kitchen floor. I fled to the doorway and stood watching while Libro put his nose to the floor, sniffed under the refrigerator, growled, and swiped. The thing stopped moving.

"Good boy!"

I gave him a biscuit. I hugged him. "You know, kiddo," I said, "now I really can't think of any reason I'd need a man in my life."

In my office, I cleaned up a week's worth of newspapers and collected Libro's toys from the floor, dropping them into their wicker basket. Contrary to my early resolve not to "spoil" him, I'd filled the basket, in a year's time, with stuffed animals of various sizes, bones of various chemically enhanced tastes, even the dreaded squeaky toys. Before I really understood that Libro was not a baby, I'd imagined him cuddling up with the plush animals— the first was a gorilla with exactly his coloring—and entertaining himself with the assortment when I wasn't there. I'd been wrong on both counts: he "killed" the gorilla by shaking it in his mouth and breaking its neck and he only played with the toys when I was present to witness or participate.

I went to my desk. Libro followed and went to his spot underneath it, right at my feet. But he was too tall to stand there now and he banged his head.

"How come you don't get it?" I said. "You've been hitting your head in the same place for a week. Go on the couch."

Shaking his head wildly, he went to the couch. I turned the computer on and checked my e-mail.

The dog community had gone on-line. Instead of abating, the war against dogs had escalated again. There had been reports of violence against dog owners who resisted being ticketed, rumors about dogs being confiscated, more angry words from the mayor and the parks commissioner. I was getting angry too at the things that had always moved me to action—people being set against each other, power being abused, and manipulation of the truth. Dogs, someone said, had become the new smokers.

Today's postings on the dogchat site asked for help placing a rottweiler found wandering in the park; advice about a landlord suddenly harassing a tenant for having a dog, and a rant about doing away with the practice of calling female dogs "bitches" when male dogs were simply called "dogs." There was also a list, with addresses, phone and fax numbers and e-mail, of people in city government opposed to dogs in the park and a call to attend a community board meeting on the subject. I wrote the date in my calendar.

I wandered to the couch, sat, opened the newspaper. Libro wriggled over and put his head in my lap. Rubbing his bad leg, feeling for the steel, my hand touched only bone. I stroked his ear. He looked up.

"I love you," I said. *"Te amo."*

He bounded off the couch, rushed to his toy basket, brought out a dark teddy bear, shook it ferociously, holding its tail in his mouth, dropped it, went back and got the squeaky lamb chop.

"You know," I said, "my idea of closeness is looking into your eyes and telling you how much I love you. Yours is jumping around with a pink plastic lamb chop."

I had the uncanny feeling I'd been there before, trapped in this same gender glitch. But that was another lifetime.

I threw the lamb chop as hard and fast as I could and a delighted Libro brought it back.